Rx Humor Care

Click Here *

(ok, try turning the pages)

Mary Bristol

Table of Contents

California Here We Go Arizona Here We Come 7

The Sedona Vortex 17

Eighteen Stories Up 26

Swamp Boat to the 35

Ritz Carlton 35

Thirty Years To Get To Epcot 43

Let's Go River Cruising 48

The Red Light District 59

Boarding the Ship, ... 66

Find the Bar 66

Grab the Quiet Boxes 74

The Doctors Onboard Are 95 years old! 82

He's Cured, We are in Nuremberg! 88

The Nurse is Sick 95

Licorice Whiskey 103

With The Monks 103

The Blue Danube, Dance with Me 109

Eighty-Five Locks 113

Making Strudel, the Right Way 117

Made in China or Budapest 122

Prague and Goodbye 127

Did We Just Buy A House? 133

Head North Young 142

Man or Old Man 142

The Five-Year Storage Locker 150

The Mall of America 156

The Lobster Race 161

High Centered on the Ice Cap 167

Establish a New Doctor, Diagnosed S.A.D. .. 174

The Polar Vortex 179

What makes me think I'm Forty? 183

We're Engaged 187

I'm a Baby Boomer Grandma 193

Understanding the X's and Y's 201

Hidden Jewels in the Consignment Store .. 207

Miss Mary, You Should Have 216

Stayed in the South 216

Surgery Again?	224
Sleeping Upright	230
Paint a Picture or The House	237
Behold All Things New	245
How Political Do You Want to Be?	250
Change is Good, I Want A Tree House	255
Rx From Me To You	262
Smack Talk	267
The Final Will	271

Dedicated to Erma Bombeck

My humor for the day, my idol, and my escape, to a funny book was the author Erma Bombeck. She wrote about life as a mother and a housewife I loved her. She has been gone eighteen years now. My youngest twenty nine year old daughter does not even recognize her name.

I will never forget Erma; she was my inspiration to write this book. That, and everyone I know say to me, "You should write a book, that was so funny." Humor is the nectar of life. Combined with a fine glass of wine... or a donut, I'm not picky.

To my husband, my family, my friends and to God...it is impossible to get through life without humor.

Follow these directions carefully. These chapters are similar to shopping on the web; reading out of order will only result in indigestion and frustration. You cannot purchase sections; it is the whole or nothing at all.

Warning, the title says it all, this book is a prescription to a dose of levity for you're well being.

Now, do not be one of those, more is better, overdosing individuals, or I will have to write another book!

                      Mary Bristol

California Here We Go
Arizona Here We Come

My husband and I raised seven children in sunny California. God knows how we did it. We didn't; we fought every day, according to our kids. They still to this day, do not know the definition of a black-white conversation. I say, "The sky is grey and cloudy," and he says, "Nope, it's sunny and clear to me." I say, "The bank account is empty" and he says, "What do you mean, its empty?" Well, there could be a shade of grey there; the bank could have twenty-two cents in it, but for purposes of living, its EMPTY!

What takes me to hysterical screaming is the question, "What do you mean?" It's a form of I can't hear you, you are babbling again. All of those exchanges over forty years, is not fighting, it is black whiting.

People would always ask me, "Seven kids, why

would you have seven kids?" "Are you Mormon, are you Catholic?" I would just smile and say, "I liked babies!" Who can criticize that? And sure enough they would always come back with the final question "Are you stupid?"

Now that question left me puzzled, and without a comeback. While it is endearing to hold a precious newborn and baby talk to it, the reality is, at that very moment in time...you give up everything on any wish list you ever had. No more cosmetics, no new underwear, no new clothes, no steak or lobster for two, you are stupid, and yes, you did it.

My friends who had only two children at the most, they were driving cars with leather seats, on their way to the spa for mani's and pedis and hot rocks applied to their spines. While I, on the other hand, was in my old station wagon stuck to the vinyl seat with some hot sticky wad of gum. Trying to get up the spine to kill the kid who always left their sack lunch somewhere in that vehicle. For every day the sack rotted, the odor would change in character. My car was a cross between a smelly locker room and the harbor fishing dock.

When the last child leaves the house, and you realize you are an empty nester, you also realize the nest is falling apart. The roof is leaking; the five layers of wallpaper you so lovingly applied is curling off, the carpet is no longer brown, it is orange. The plumbing is not working, tree roots have grown around the sewer pipe, and a ditch digger is required. Brown water is coming out of the faucets, a gaseous odor follows the brown water, no amount of Lysol will decontaminate that situation.

You are boiling water to take a bath; the lifetime guarantee on the water heater is from a company no longer in existence. At the twenty-year mark, that tank blew up and exploded all over the garage. The enthusiasm to keep up with the Jones has faded, the Jones left years ago.

It is time to sell and hit the road! "Someone is

going to love this place," I said to the realtor. "The neighborhood is wonderful, the houses so comfortable, the trees are mature and we have plums we share with the neighbors." "Just a little TLC and the buyers will have a dream home." The realtor said, "It's depreciated, you can only get a buck ninety-eight for it!" "List anyway."

I called the moving companies for an estimate. They don't come out to your home to do the estimate; you are directed to the Internet and their website. Follow the yellow brick road and click on what applies. Do you have a sofa? What size? How many cushions? Is it a hide-a-bed, Murphy bed or cot? A month later, I had the form filled in, and it tallied up the damage.

One more question, do you want us to pack or you self pack? Are you up to this, how old are you? Do you have medical insurance? Finally the conclusion, you are accepted, and pay here is the next prompt. Your 401K balances should cover this move. Our movers will be at your house at 6:00 am on the pick-up date. Be ready for them, coffee is nice, they need full access to your refrigerator and the bathroom.

The day had come; we were semi-retiring and moving to Arizona. Bruce needed to keep his finger on the pulse of his work, so we will move close to where he will continue working; I'm the one semi-retired.

At 120 degrees in the shade, if you need to commute to work, the drive should be close by. With that in mind, we found a ranch for sale near his work.

The house was typical Arizona ranch style; the driveway formed a circle of gravel allowing you to jump out and run for the front door. The doors were a wooden arch with the center of the arch about five feet from the ground; both Bruce and I suffered frontal concussions for the first month of living there.

The floors were "Mexican Paver Tile." That's a red tile with a hump in the middle of the tile. As soon as you step on it your ankle twists, and you are on crutches leapfrogging from tile to tile for six weeks.

The ceilings were low, and the windows had a windowsill depth of about three feet of adobe plaster.   This is to keep the house cool and dark. The kitchen had a window looking out to the deep lava rock swimming pool. The realtor raved about that pool; apparently, it stayed cool. As opposed to the pools in town. "Those are small and require bags of ice to cool them down," she said. "Bags of ice?" I inquired. "Yes, they buy them at the grocery store, fill up the truck and race home to throw in the pool!"

This house was one of the few in the area with a real lawn. There was a push mower in the garage, or "you can get a goat," she said. No lawn service would come out that far to the ranch. "Not a problem we like to mow the lawn, good exercise," Bruce said to her. When was the last time he saw someone in heat prostration?

We had luxury in this property, a ten-acre horse ranch with no horses, and a lava swimming pool for an evening dip. It had two air conditioners, that was comforting and it is true, the sunsets are spectacular. However, do not think you can just sit out on the pool deck and admire the sunset. The rattlesnakes have the same idea.

During the day, the heat is a blast furnace and the bees use the swimming pool for they're cool off, buzz by. They came in swarms and landed on the blue water, turning the entire pool black for the day. At about sunset, they took off, leaving behind only the ones who drowned. After an hour of pool vacuuming, it was possible to take an evening dip, however; it was necessary to swim with a flashlight clenched between your teeth, there were the scorpions, some ugly brown lizards and a few rattlesnakes which wanted to have a drink at the end of the day. Bruce swam in between them; I took a shower inside with a black light at the ready.

The realtor did mention the scorpions but considered them a nuisance rather than a venomous killer. The baby ones are the lethal ones, "Don't be afraid of the big ones.", she said. "They don't bite, she said, they sting and they ambush their prey. "Get a black light and check the closets in the daytime," she said. Put that on the grocery list, whatever it is. I called the bug man for weekly service.

That same real estate lady who had lived there thirty years and just didn't think they were an issue, called one day. She said she had been hospitalized with her leg the size of an elephant from a scorpion that just happened to be in her bed sheets. They were considering amputation; I thought she should have had a lobotomy.

I started checking the closets. I wondered if the pain in my legs, the muscle twitching of my eyelids, the increased heart palpitations, as I checked every closet, was due to fear. Or, had I been stung by a baby scorpion and didn't even know it. Maybe I'm the one that needed the lobotomy for being out on the ranch in the first place.

My first time I encountered a rattle snack; I tried to think of what the first aid book said. Don't move, I didn't. Don't shout, I couldn't. Don't wet your pants, they will hear it. I did!! But, I did pack a gun and I did shoot that coiled reptile squarely between the eyes! I did not keep the rattler for a keepsake; I left that snake for the desert food chain. Something would come along and eat it. Or else, someone would think it a rare delicacy and snatch it right up for Sunday dinner.

I told Bruce not to buy rattlesnake boots; I'll shoot first, and ask questions later.

Scottsdale is the shopping Mecca for the Phoenix area; I managed to buy turquoise jewelry, a suede leather jacket with fringe, boots and pottery all while living in Arizona. The question is, where will I ever wear that jacket, that Indian jewelry and set the table in adobe pottery again? It has its look, and it stays in Arizona. A woman dripping in turquoise with a fringed suede jacket in Florida is a showstopper bordering on mental.

Golf is big in Arizona, man will not empty the trash, but he will get up at 4:00 AM to be on the golf course. He will sustain third degree sunburn, heat prostration, and dehydration before he will give in to the Arizona heat and get off the course.

Women golfers turn into old hides out there on the desert. They start their first year of retirement golfing at age 65 and end the second year looking about 105 in age. The women run to the spas to be oiled and steamed and kid themselves, that sun isn't puckering their faces into prunes.

A badge of honor though, at cocktail hour, they are all in short skirts, and they don't care what their poor puckered bodies look like, they all look the same. Lemon yellow or lime green cheerleader skirts! Time is reversing. Rah, Rah, Rah, Sis boom

The Sedona Vortex

My girlfriend Patty, from California and I took a few days for a girl's retreat in Sedona. She goes at the usual fast pace of any Southern Californian, so gearing her down to a medium roar is difficult. We felt Sedona could give us inner peace, relaxation, a natural tan.

After checking into the timeshare condo welcome center, (a timeshare condo is a pre-purchased short stay for $85,000, extrapolated out to make you think it is only $59 a day, all amenities included). We were instructed to take a short walk outside at 119 degrees, to the entertainment and sales office building to pick up the keys!

Following the two hour presentation, "short welcome speech" to buy yet another time-share, we were given the keys to the condo.

By then, exhaustion had set in, and we missed the

vortex sunset, it was pitch dark, and we were on our own to navigate the property and find building E, upstairs condo 588. There was no elevator in building E only available in A, B, C, and D; as we didn't buy the condo.

This happened to Bruce and me in Puerto Vallarta, Mexico one time too. We went to their two-hour (short presentation) of their new property outside of the city, in exchange for a Mexican Fiesta buffet dinner that night at 6:00 pm. We were transported to a new property condo timeshares in luxury air conditioned bus, complete with tour guide and bottles of tequila with that little worm in the bottle. Everyone thought that was great and chugged it down, I let my worm go in the bus.

But then when we didn't sign on the dotted line for a limited, fast selling timeshares, there was no bus for transport back to our hotel. We stood on the dirt road and waited for what the locals called the "chicken bus". A sawed off roof of a school bus, with a rack on top for the cages of live chickens, climb aboard, no one spoke English, but they were all laughing. Those Gringos didn't buy the timeshare!! That chicken bus arrived back at the hotel at 8:30 pm in time for last night's hard dinner rolls and bottled water.

On this retreat, I realized I was on my own with my two suitcases packed at my usual one hundred pounds each. Patty had her husband pack her suitcase. He rolls her clothes into paper towel holders, lined up symmetrically in her carry on. She can exist for weeks out of those paper towel holders. She doesn't even recycle them; she tosses them and has less weight in her carry on suitcase for her souvenirs. There is no point to that packing, if your souvenirs are mini size earrings and post cards.

I went to a gemstone rock show and bought the hoax Zircon crystal formation that weighs fifty pounds. Stunning for the living room glass coffee table.

That is a mistake if the glass tabletop is rated to

hold ten pounds. My gemstone souvenir crashed through the glass tabletop, landed on the rug in millions of shattered flakes and shards. I then attempted to vacuum it up with the newly purchased ball rolling vacuum cleaner. The warranty does not cover fake rock damage. They should put that vacuum through a few more trial studies; this could happen to anyone!

There was always sunrise and another scorcher day to find our inner peace. We were on our retreat; we were not going to prepare dinner in that condo's fully equipped kitchen of a microwave, popcorn popper and wine bottle opener.

We set out to find a Sedona culinary delight that first evening. Before traveling with any companion, check your dining habits with each other. Are you a hole in the wall diner or do you frequent the Ritz? It helps when you are choosing your dining experiences.

That night, the only restaurant open was the hole

in the wall cafe, serving last night veal cutlet. That was a recipe for Ptomaine poisoning. However, if your mouth isn't stinging and you are not nauseous, and it is the only place to get food; it's ok, go ahead and eat the blue plate special.

We talked about the energy vortex climb the next day. We believed we did believe in the unbelievable. That night after the dry crusted veal dinner special, we returned to the condo to have a spa tub bath.

I brought all the bath bubble I could find, bath salts, bath oils and a rubber duck. I was ready to fire that gigantic tub up and relax. My friend chose a glass of wine and a book; she passed on the spa treatment. Soon, my tub was overflowing with bubbles, bubbles that I could not see over, bubbles that I could not make go away and finally VORTEX bubbles. I was afraid and called out for my friend. She has never gotten over the bubble bath rescue; she also has never traveled with me again.

The next morning Patty wanted breakfast. Did I say, I don't eat breakfast? Patty does, and it needs to include eggs. It was a risk, but we found another hole in the wall cafe and she was having her corn beef and hash with an egg resting on top, blue plate special. I went all out and had coffee with hazelnut cream and a cinnamon roll the size of a dinner plate. Carbs for the climb, I could walk off those few calories!

We had to get walking sticks, a must in Arizona, so said the guy who made them out of cactus twigs and sold them for $90 each. We followed the map and set out to find the energy vortex. Of course, just like hunting deer, one must go up the hill, the spiritual energy is always up. So up we went, over rocks, down we went, over rocks. Patty was skipping along at a brisk pace, and I was huffing and puffing to keep up.

At one point, I begged her to stop and survey the area. I asked her, "If this vortex experience is an inner dimensional experience, couldn't we take a chance that it might be inside the car also? She did not seem to make my connection of an inner spirit thought. So I told her I just saw a rattlesnake under a rock. She blazed a trail back to the car. You do what you have to do.

On to the Grand Canyon tour. Everyone goes to the Grand Canyon but do they book the train get-a-way, complete with the Baron Suite and all you can eat buffet after you disembark the train? Well, I did.

We've never been backpackers; this tour was our first backpacking experience.

We were to start at the top of the canyon and plan on the entire day for the grand tour and then a descent into the floor of the canyon. I think you should learn from other people's experiences. I do faithfully watch the "Surviorman" on TV and file to memory his fire building skills; his complete salads prepared in between poison ivy; he amazes me.

I packed the first backpack with quart bottles of

water, cans of pork'n'beans in case we got lost, flashlights, fire making supplies, kindling, sleeping bags, portable toilet and shower, and a heavy-duty ax. That was in Bruce's backpack.

My backpack had rain poncho's (it might), shampoo, conditioner, battery operated curling iron, extra clothes, handy wipes, bathing wipes, quilted toilet paper, my little bag of cosmetics and a few zip bags of candy and cookies. We took the beginner trail and failed as Junior Hiker's. It was embarrassing.

However, I did not expect to end up with a donkey as my means of transportation down a shelf on a trail. The guide said I had on "Musk perfume" and the donkey wanted to mate with me instead of carry me to the bottom of the canyon. No refunds on that tour, just walk back up the cliff in shame. Bruce carried on for days that he could have done it; he could have made that little donkey hold him up for three hours. We hadn't even made it to the weighing station; we would have flunked that too.

If I had a dime for every time, someone said to me. "Oh, you will love Arizona, it's a dry heat." A women's body should not resemble beef jerky out of the dehydrator; that is dry heat!

The entire time we were in Arizona, I searched for Erma's house or grave. I knew she was buried under a 29,000-pound rock. I was going to turn over every single one of them, until I found her. And then, I realized she is buried in Ohio. I'll get there, Erma.

Eighteen Stories Up

When we moved to Florida for another one of Bruce's jobs, I was excited. I was going to get to see Disney World, Epcot and Cape Canaveral. Maybe not in the summer, it's a WET hot there! Meaning, you get up in the morning, take a shower to cool off, stand by the air conditioner to get dressed, stay inside and hibernate. Or, go out and within minutes, your clothes are soaked, your hair is flat, and your energy is sapped.

Another real estate lady assuring us that they don't have scorpions in Florida. They do have no- see - ums!! They attack morning noon and night, and you cannot see them, only feel them somewhere on your body. So where are they? I called the bug service, "Give me a twice weekly service, I have a black light, will that help?" No, they said, "Get a battery operated fly swatter, and you can hear them fry!"

I can remember when you bought a fly swatter at the grocery store for 49 cents, that tennis racket battery operated insect controller was $29.95! The holes in the electric net were too big for the no-see- um's, but if you swung toward your face and hit your nose, it would fry it to a well-done state.

To live at the beach in Florida is to live in a high-rise condo complex. Those buildings are made of cinder block cement, built to withstand the weekly hurricane coming through, at will. Bruce and I have always been first floor ground people. When we were shown the condo on the eighteenth floor, it all seemed normal until we stepped off the elevator on the eighteenth floor, and you are not inside the building.

The walkway and entrance doors to all of the condo's are accessed from outside of the building. A shelf of cement protruding from the wall of the building with an open railing, what holds that up? I don't feel secure even with re-bar when I'm on a gantry in the direct line to a space shuttle.

Our perky real estate lady started out onto that walkway. Bruce followed her, stopping occasionally to hang over the railing and survey the parking lot below. I froze in place; it was a "Depends" moment!

How would I carry groceries and find my door? I would need to be pre-medicated with an anti-anxiety medication just to get off the elevator; I don't handle drugs well. I was shouting my questions to this woman as she was opening the door to the condo all the way down that walkway. "Is there a way, from say, the roof, which I could just fall into my condo unit without walking this green mile?" She laughed, "You'll get used to it!"

Ambulances were constantly flashing red and blue lights going down the streets and sirens going off, I know why now. Seniors were splattered all over those parking lots, and they hadn't even gotten into their cars, they fell off the shelf.

I shimmied along the inside wall until I could get to the door and look at the inside the condo. This place had to be of male architectural design. The kitchen was in the center of the floor plan, a dark dungeon, no windows on any wall. It was so dark in there; we couldn't find the light switch. All of us formed a single line, hand on the shoulder, and shuffled around the room until we found one.

Once we turned on the lights; we could find our way to the bedroom. And then there was abundant light, a wall with a large sliding glass door opening onto a balcony. Strange, the wrought iron fence was about four inches from the glass door.

My shoe size is 10, what was the builder thinking might step out onto that balcony, a pet turtle? No dog of any size could run out there in the mornings, a cat could traverse sideways. However, the birds didn't fly up that high, so what would be the point for the cat? Fresh air maybe, not in Florida, it is 100% humidity, at eighteen stores you are in the clouds! My best guess was a surplus run on sliding doors, and they just hung a four-inch balcony on for code requirements.

There was another balcony increasing to about three feet wide off the living room, just enough space to take a swan dive off of that banister and jettison you in the 200-degree hot tub eighteen stories down.

The sea gulls flew by every morning. If I was sitting out there with a cup of coffee, those birds flew in a straight line, turned their heads to me, eyeballed me, eye to eye and we bonded. They don't befriend a pilot at that altitude; the jet engine is their demise. All of the other ladies in the building were bonding with the sea gulls, I could see no harm in it, except maybe for the days the cloud cover was low.

A sea gull would get off course; cruise into the glass patio door and splat to his death. Those ambulance sirens would go off, bird lovers and avid bird watchers can't take that drama, and we had a heart attack on our hands!

After living right next to the Pacific Ocean, in California for twenty years, watching the surfers in blue water, and the whales migrate to Mexico, this view was bland. This Atlantic Ocean was a large grey colored pond of water with ripple size waves for as far as you could see.

If I held a pair of binoculars, I could catch a glimpse of a cruise ship headed out to sea. If I invested in a Chilian Alma telescope, I could watch people get dressed for dinner.

We had excitement one day when I stepped out onto the balcony for my morning cup of coffee, looked down to the beach, and there was a crowd of five hundred people looking at a shipwreck! I ran for the binoculars, after all it was eighteen stories down! Two beach sheriff deputies, with drawn guns, and an empty rowboat! Those morning bloody Mary's in Florida distort things, somebody thought it was the sister Concordia and called that right into 911.

Would you believe the Florida golfers were up at 4:00 am and out in that wet, oppressive heat.? They will schlep through the tall grass, fight the bugs, and step on small green lizards to chase that golf ball. They conserve energy by being in a fringed golf cart and pink shirts, with flaps on their backs. They take their fluid IV, I guess. Nothing deters them; they ride on airboats across the swamp with alligators to get to that ninth hole!

I didn't even see women golfers in Florida. They gathered at the condo complex pool for morning exercise and screwdrivers, followed by midmorning tanning and vodka tonics. Then they met the boys for lunch and martinis, back to the clubhouse for bridge and BYOB's. It's pretty quiet on the eighteenth floor at 5:00 PM; everyone in the building was drunk and is in bed.

There are no official Floridians; they are all transplants from New Jersey, New York, New Hampshire, Massachusetts, and once and a while, a Mainer. They click together joined by their native state.

If you mention, you were once from California; they disable the elevator, and you can't get home.

We changed our license plates to South Dakota, and they loved us. "Mount Rushmore, do you live there?"

"It's a mountain people! There are no cul de sac's at the base of Mount Rushmore!"

Home Owners Association will not be part of our life after Bruce' retirement work ends, and we settle in to conclude our life, somewhere in the USA. The rules these people dream up at the monthly meeting at the clubhouse, border on psychotic.

Always the President of the association is some guy who did not want to retire, they walked him out the door. If man cannot put the toilet seat down at his own house, why would man dream up a parking spot and measure the distance the front bumper of your car to the nearest bush. If closer than six inches, you are ticketed.

If you receive more than three tickets, you lose your right to park anywhere within a five-mile radius. If you have had hip surgery; however, you can park within one mile.

Could we send this guy to Siberia and make him use the outhouse?

Swamp Boat to the Ritz Carlton

Before the trip to Europe, there was no reason we couldn't explore Florida. We started with the swamp airboat ride. I don't recommend this to anyone who has a fear of water, alligators or cares about the $200 they spent on getting a hair coloring and style job.

That kid running the boat, lied to me, I told him I preferred not to get wet, and he said, "Take those upper seats, you'll be fine", until he turned the boat over!!

We paid a fortune to wheeze through the Everglades, swatting unknown bugs, hanging on for dear life, only to come roaring back to the dock without seeing anything in the brochure and soaking wet with swamp water. No one said to have a water purifier straw hung around our neck in case we gulped the swamp water, the boat guy said, I wouldn't get wet! Swamp water fever, the only cure, is death. Those brochures do not disclose what could be...and they don't hire boat guys that tell the truth!

After I had recuperated from the airboat ride, we continued on driving across the state to the Seminole Indian Reservation. Bruce did this in South Dakota; he got us onto the Oglala Indian reservation, and we couldn't get out of it. Hours went by with only our car on a dirt road, barbed wire fences and old tires hanging on the fences, with lettering saying NO TRESPASSING!

How does he manage to always get us on an Indian Reservation that we don't know how to get off?

This time on the Seminole Reservation we ended up driving through a burial grounds. Now that is not a good thing. If he wouldn't keep looking down at the GPS screen and veering off to the side of the road as he does, he wouldn't have hit one of those posts and Chief "SO and So" wouldn't have fallen on top of our car hood, wrapped in blankets. How would we get him back up on that bed in the sky they call a gravesite?

By the time I worked all of this out in my head, he was through the reservation and headed for the Ritz Carlton in Naples.

Checking into a Ritz Carlton in Naples, after traveling through the swamp is tricky at best. We had to get past the bellman, which thought we were vagrants from the beach, odd smelling ones at that; you could just tell by the look on his face. A hundred dollar bill will get you to the desk.

I was in an apologetic mode to a receptionist who could care less; her head was facing down into the computer screen and she was in up sell mode. "We have a penthouse suite with eight rooms and seven bathrooms, four king beds, would you like to upgrade to that?" "Really my dear, can you see I'm soaked in swamp water, is there a shower in a regular room, good to go, I'll take my original reservation, thank you."

As soon as the bellman dropped our luggage off at the room, I was on the phone to room service. This swamp muck will take some serious soaking. I need sustenance.

"Hello, room service, bring me a double cheeseburger, fries, and a chocolate coke." I would be fine after my bath, "did you want anything honey?" Knowing full well he is going to say, no. He hates to pay 18% gratuity, 20% added gratuity to run it up to the room and another in hand tip at the door. If I'm doing it anyway, why doesn't he just add a burger, he's going to be eating half of mine as he say's, "I just want a bite!"

Sometimes, when a person is covered with mud, they stand their ground and protect their burger by locking themselves in the bathroom and play loud music! "Did you say something dear?"

The weekend we ventured off to historic St Augustine was in celebration of our 30 something Anniversary. If I had to give birth to seven children, can I not expect him to remember their birthdays and our Anniversary? I hardly remember those birthdays; I only associate pain with them. The Anniversary date is the same rationale that a date started all the birth dates. He should remember them. With that in mind, Anniversaries are to celebrate my sticking it out and should be "done up brown."

The excursion to St Augustine was set up to be a romantic get-a-way, again from the no- see- ums and love bugs. Seems the love bugs got their start in St Augustine, the college kids let them out of the science lab and they propagated by the billions.

Our room in the historic hotel downtown was the "Love Birds Nest", located on the fourth floor when there was no fourth floor that would be the roof. First you climbed a flight of stairs straight up to the bed floor, then another flight of stairs to the toilet room floor and finally another flight of stairs to the heart shaped Jacuzzi tub floor.

Trouble was, no one had booked that love nest

since the hotel maintenance changed the old lead water pipes to PVC plastic. The maintenance guys changed the pipes out and left the roof. No one tested to see if the water would work and no one ran the water to see what would jettison out of that faucet when you did get ready for the "Love tub".

Gusts of air and brown water full of black love bugs spewed from the brass faucet, the birds outside could hear me scream. Bruce called the front desk for help; the staff didn't know how to get to that tub room. A bottle of Champagne and hot dipped strawberries are not going to make me forget that tub water.

Move me to the penthouse at the Ritz! Never mind it is a twelve-hour drive away, I can only stand so much.

Someone my age is not going to go to St Augustine and not take in the Fountain of Youth. They sell the water from the fountain in quart bottles. I brought my own whiskey barrel for refill. Bruce always wants to know where I am going to put whatever it is that I buy. "Are you kidding me, that barrel has a sacred spot on your side of the bed." "I need it, do you know that Botox is formaldehyde?" "This is natural homeopathic, from the deep dark well, cure for my aging." "I will find a home for the barrel of youth."

It did seem strange a bunch of old wrinkled ladies were selling it. Odd sales and marketing, I still believed it would work.

I'm still squeezing the wood for the last drop of moisture in that barrel; no results yet to the facial wrinkles, however, I think my ear lobes look nice.

Finally, there's the issue of the Florida oranges. We drove from the top of Florida to the bell at Key West and from Fort Lauderdale to the other side of Florida at Tampa, no orange trees. I never saw an orange tree, not even in anyone's yard with the pink plastic Flamingo's. No oranges!

In California, you drive through orchards of avocados, you can get out and mash the ones on the ground and have your guacamole.

In Hawaii, those pineapples are grown right up to the side of the road, pick one up, no one would ever know. In Idaho, you are wondering if you will ever get out of the potato fields. But Florida, where are the oranges? If they come from China, I give up!

If you have to take an air swamp boat to get to the fields of oranges, I will not do that again; I won't even watch the show on TV with the guy wrestling the alligator in the swamp.

He's drinking that water; it's a given, Swamp Water Fever, he dies!

Thirty Years To Get To Epcot

We were married in Pensacola, Florida at the Naval Air Station chapel, the year doesn't matter, it's the fact we did it. They were just building Epcot in Disney World; it was about to open when we moved to California. We shall return were our last words! It has been thirty years and now we are seniors!

I investigated the specials for seniors to go see the park. There are no specials or discounts; ten years old plus are all the same price!

Somebody forgot to inform the marketing department, the senior has the credit card! The ten year old is the bouncing, cut in front of you," I wanna ride the Matterhorn", twenty times consecutively, little twit. That age group has no respect for the senior who has waited thirty years to see this place!

The most that kid is going to eat is an $8 corn dog,

a $15 funnel cake and a $12 disgusting cherry, lime, root beer drink. That drink is disguised in a $15 space ship container; with an led light and a button he can push and spray the senior with that sticky mess.

Whereas, the senior woman shells out the big bucks every thirty minutes. Grandma wants to taste the round the world experience! And because she had to spend precious time in the restroom half bathing and hand spotting her designer leisure suit from that spaceship bomb explosion of multicolored sugar water, she won't be offering anything to that little darling.

She's known at her hometown zoo for carrying a bag of quarters so the little kids can feed the pellet machine and toss the food to the goats. Not this time, she's in survival mode.

She will start the morning at Mickey's character breakfast buffet, thirty minutes later; she is ready for Cuban coffee and pastry. Another thirty minutes and she's at the 50's ice cream parlor.

Lunch at the China Palace, 30 minutes later (that Chinese food just doesn't fill you up), she is ready for Wolfgang's sliders. Then there is afternoon high tea at the Garden Tea Room, another stop at the Brown Derby for a sandwich. She may take a nap on a park bench for about an hour and then she's up and ready to stop at the story time cafe for a hot fudge sundae. She'll try the Gelato, and she will still be ready for fine dining before the fireworks!

If the park gave her senior discount, she would buy just about everything she paws through in the gift shops. She has the credit card!! Big mistake people, keep your seniors happy with the dollar discount.

Walt's park is full of senior citizens. If anyone dares gripe about their wheelchairs and umbrellas with sharp metal tips, it is for self-preservation. It is their protection against the young parent with the motorized three-wheeler stroller that has wheels weighing 50 pounds each. That wheel running across your foot or ramming into you hip

is automatic surgery when you arrive back home!
We will not be deterred; we will see the
amusement parks and ride whatever is within our
medical boundaries. George Bush Senior sky dives
on his birthday, these rides are nothing compared
to that!

My husband cannot accept his age; he is in line
with those kids for the most thrilling ride they can
bring on. Watching him come out the exit line is
an automatic 911 call.

I warned him, the signs said, "Don't do this if you
have white hair", but oh no, he is forever twenty.
I just up the accidental death and dismemberment
policies before we travel to kid's amusement parks.

The hotel package turned out to be another time-
share condo, who knew, not me? Online hotel
booking can get you into trouble sometimes.

This package advertised the hotel room, admission
to the park for one day and free parking! The
admission to the park part was if we signed up and

bought another time-share,. The free parking was because the hotel was eighty miles from Disney World, and you had to ride a shuttle bus, traverse a swamp in a boat and arrive in the park on the monorail.

It was dark and time for the fireworks before we got into the park!

Heck of a package price though!

Let's Go River Cruising

For a vacation treat while we were in Florida, and before we had even explored Disney World or Epcot, I decided we should take a European riverboat cruise at Christmas time.

It sounded like an opportunity to flee the no- see-ums and Love Bugs, have a White Christmas in Europe. We could start an around the world adventure. Done, "book um Dano."

I had never been on a cruise, we had a stateroom with a balcony, I packed for the three weeks with the thought the extra luggage I could sit out on the balcony, if need be.

Who are these people who can travel with just a carry-on bag? In spite of the fact my large suitcase weighed in at fifty pounds on the nose, a carry- on, weighing approximately the same and a purse I use at flea markets for maximum capacity, I still forgot my underwear.

I think those who can travel for three weeks in a small carry on are living in paper clothes and pulling them out of a suitcase like a Kleenex box.

I decided I could just buy underwear as I travel through Germany. Dessous is the German word for undergarment, now to the size? My hips do not translate to anything except too many pies. My translator machine does not size underwear.

I would just wash my undies out each night and perfume the rinse water.

I made checklists until I was blue in the face. I checked the airline baggage criteria, and I was set to go. I labeled and scanned, and I notified the bank, the credit card companies, and sat around thinking, what if the plane falls out of the sky, I better have a plan.

I established a separate travel account; I reserved lots in Rosecrans cemetery back home, just in case.

I also had to tell myself, this Christmas; Santa was delivering envelopes to the kids, not packages.

I am the queen of packages, how to cull down to an envelope?. When we got back home from a Christmas trip, I double checked the mailbox drawer at the Post Office; no packages sent to us from the kids that year, no envelopes either, I don't think they received this new method of Christmas very well.

When we took our three youngest children to London for Christmas one year (we were out of home due to mold and Santa had a huge guilt complex). We had our share of unusual moments, with fifteen pieces of luggage, all five of us scrambled to grab our suitcases, at the baggage claim.

When the belt stopped, and the last suitcase had been retrieved, one of our girls was sobbing. Her suitcases were gone, never to be seen again, months later she got a check for $13, depreciation!

It was London in the winter; it was fairly cold. She didn't want to carry her coat, so she put her coat in her suitcase! I couldn't believe it, wasn't it at all obvious to anyone, if you have your coat on your body, they cannot steal it from you.

Off to Harrods's to shop for everything for her, the children's department had cricket uniforms, it was a different look for her. She maintains to this day; she was traumatized from the experience, and it was our entire fault. I beg to differ, I had my coat on, if I had lost my bag, I could have survived in a cable knit jumpsuit, if I just had to.

So...with those memories in mind, I believe this trip was well on its way to being absolutely flawless. On to the airport in Miami, we arrived the three hours early for International flights, only to be told, the airlines desk would not be open for another hour.

Some fool designed benches to sit on at that airport, which looked like padded boomerangs.

They had no backs to them; just straddle the thing for an hour. "What happened to chairs?"

The cattle guard barriers were finally put in place. I glanced over to the First Class line. Interesting, there was a young woman with a baby about eight weeks old in a stroller designed to resemble a mini Lexus. All I could think of was times have changed, here I am a senior for my first trip to Amsterdam, and she travels with a new baby in First Class. First Class on this airline had beds!!

Then the Business Class people, all extremely young, I don't mean young executives, I mean tattooed kids, giggling and shoving their way to the front of the line. What businesses are they in? It looks like drug trafficking, however, the dogs were sniffing me? Why is a drug sniffing dog always what I call a crotch dog, there are other areas of the body one could stash drugs.

Economy Class, that's us! I had to twist Bruce's arm to put five dollars in the machine and get a luggage cart. He tries to stack two large bags with two carry-ons' and his backpack and my purse all behind himself, stacked on top of one suitcase. Then he can't understand why they all come apart.

At that point, he is blaming the luggage manufacturer, "poor design!" I just follow along behind him and pick up whatever comes flying my way, there is no sense in trying to find logic to his travel style.

We started getting the bags weighed; the big ones passed with flying colors! Then, they spotted our carry-on's. "Oh no," the attendant said. " NO," we could not have two carry-on's. The airline website said we could, but they had just changed the rule.

We now had the option, go back to the shops and buy a big suitcase and condense the two carry-on's in it and pay an extra hundred dollars. Or, "Take out what you don't want, give it to the person behind you in line and pay a hundred dollars for both bags."

That carry on of mine is a Tommy Bahamas, do I

want to chuck it or pay for it? Bruce was in shock mode. He wanted his new headsets, and our nifty battery operated massaging pillows, in his backpack, so he said, and I quote, "check them through". Ok, but this is going very fast, are you sure?

Now, we were ticketed and have a boarding pass ready for TSA. Just as we are standing in a cattle guard line for security, I was thinking about the advanced plan he insisted on that I go through first and catch the carry-on. One of them had our new notebook computer!

He rationalized, he would probably be delayed with my nebulizer machine for my asthma; they have to have a dog sniff it and tag it that we are not blowing up the plane with it.

I started thinking; I have to unzip these boots, not lose my balance and break something and catch that computer, when all of a sudden I realized it was on its way to the bowels of the plane in one of the carry- on bags. I turned around and told him the computer was checked through with the carry-on's, along with his medicines and my JEWELRY! He started emitting some smoke from his ears, and his face was cherry red, "What to do?"

Stop at Starbucks and think about it, decompress. Sitting next to use was another couple our age decompressing also.. She was traumatized her Brighton bag had to be checked with the regular luggage; it had her medicines and her JEWELRY! Like minds here, don't tell the kids, they will think we are senile!

We are in the 330 Air bus, two seats in one row, then four or five in the middle section, then two more in another row. The cruise line set up our airline arrangements; we are 36 E and F, which is in the middle of the middle row!

I'm sorry, but I don't think there is enough space for a Nat, much less my body. I gave Bruce the aisle seat so he could stretch his legs. I didn't know where mine were supposed to go. I finally packed myself into my seat, bent forward just as the guy in front of me reclined his seat, which caused me to become wedged in a fetal position.

I started crying for help, Bruce had already put his headset on; he could hear nothing. I thought he realized my predicament, he was turning red again, and it was because his headset had dead batteries.

He finally looked over to me, to confiscate my headset. I had about enough oxygen left to whisper to him, "Here's the deal buddy; I get a working one, you have the aisle seat."

When the lights came on, and we were descending into Zurich, I thought of all the years I had wanted to see Switzerland. Trouble is if you cannot see out of the plane, and your legs are in a fixed cramp, you just ask the person next to you if they would mind describing it to you. Our plane was late arriving; I didn't know what the pilots were doing all night long, but they did have a tail wind. I thought that speeded up the process, I read that in an airplane magazine at the dentist's office.

We had five minutes until boarding the next flight, just enough time to find a restroom. It was like a spaceship in there; all modern Danish design, stark white, chrome fixtures, and frosted milk glass doors.

I could not figure out how to open the door to the "water closet." I couldn't figure out how to flush the square command panel. With four buttons written in Swiss German, what all could this toilet do?

That second button was a Bidet, with ice water! Had I pushed the third button I later learned, it was in Islamic and a recording would come on saying a prayer. "Praise be to Allah, who relieved me of the filth and gave me relief." I could not get the door open to get out.

Try explaining that experience to a Swiss Air agent rolling her eyes at me for being the last person to board. I asked Bruce if he had a restroom like that, and of course, he replied, "What do you mean, ice water Bidet?" "What's a Bidet?"

On to Amsterdam, I tried to look out the airplane window and see the beauty of the mountains and the snow covered land and my eyes just failed shut on me. No sleep will do that to you, maybe those chocolates they hand out are laced with something?

When we arrived, I told Bruce the cruise line would have a car and driver waiting for us, but he decided to go look for him and there I was with another wagon full of luggage, and no husband.

I have a term for his "I'll do it my way," I call it alternate plan B. If GPS has routed him to a destination, he has the alternate plan B and invariably we end up on a dead end street.

The Red Light District

Wherever a woman travels, she observes the dress of other women; there is a code to follow. If you wear a fur fluff hat in Amsterdam, I have to have one. Do not do this at the red light district, it does not apply, approaching the area is like the summer solstice in Seattle, naked people everywhere.

In the dining room of the hotel is fair game. People looked strange to me. They looked like they were going out to clean out the garage rather than sightseeing in Amsterdam. I had put careful thought into the attire, and they distorted my image at breakfast. Next time I go to Amsterdam, I'll just wear my "Let's get Crackin" hoodie from Maine.

The buffet of Danish food that morning resembled a football party spread. Cold cuts, cheese boards, hard fruit and hard cooked eggs, breads so dense, you need a forklift to put then on your plate. I'm not a breakfast person, so I headed for the coffee bar and ate more chocolates; cheese is not a jump-start for me.

My husband acted like he had been raised there and filled his plate to the brim ate everything and never even commented that there was no cereal, pancakes or scrambled eggs. He shoved an extra hard boiled egg in his coat and was good to go.

It was a blizzard outside, and we were expected to walk several blocks to the train station. Had I booked lower steerage and didn't know it?

The snow came down so hard; we could see nothing. Bruce does not ask for directions; he just keeps on going. This is a foreign country, where will we end up? The answer. The red light district, by airborne smell alone.

I am very sensitive to any drug; second hand pot smoke, is like an inhalation treatment to me. I was staggering, slurring my speech, laughing and hungry for anything edible. I was high!

We stopped at a hotel and found their dining room and a fireplace. I ordered everything on the menu; I ate mine, Bruce's plate of food, and the plate of food from the lady at the table next to us. She left her food to go to the bathroom; she loses! Bruce was humiliated and threatened not to take me to the Anne Frank House, I shaped up fast.

We are the only tourists to skip the red light district, due to Mom being high on second hand pot! I will never know what the window hookers looked like; I'll never know if my fur hat would have been a street corner signal, I'll never see a bong. I missed Amsterdam's red light district, all because a group of juvenile delinquents walked right next to me and "Pot-highed me!"

All I have to remember Amsterdam is a pair of wooden Dutch shoes and a set of antique ice skates that I bought at a corner flea market. Bruce wouldn't let me go into the shops because of my staggering. I was incognito at the flea market; everyone else was staggering too.

The city is filled with maniac bicyclists, rows of bicycles chained to anything solid. However, we were there in December. You just don't think a sliding bicycle on a street of ice in a snow blizzard will be your demise.

Between the pot smokers, the bicycles coming from all directions, train tracks that criss cross one another and trains going two different directions, it was safer to watch from my room in the hotel. But then the Anne Frank House was calling me.

I had to brave the elements and go. I had private entrance VIP tickets I bought online. The tickets did not tell you where the private entrance was, and everything is written in Dutch, so they were useless, we just stood in the cattle guard line and waited it out like the rest of the poor fools in the blizzard.

Once we were inside the house that would have been the downstairs store and we made our way to the staircase to the living quarters the Frank family stayed in during that time. It was obvious the movie didn't capture everything.

The stairs were about eighteen inches wide, and vertical was hardly the word for it, straight up with stair treads about four inches wide. Since we were still in the cattle guard line of people,; that aligns your face in someone else's rear end with a panic sensation coming over everyone.

It is a known fact middle age people do not have eighteen-inch hips. If even one percent of those people climbing that staircase were as claustrophobic as I am, then there was bound to be a road kill jam up. And I would be the killer!

The rooms were void of any furnishing, not even a bench for an asthmatic to try and recover the climb there, so I made Bruce into a chair position and sat on him until I could breathe again.

And then I looked at every picture; touched everything I wasn't suppose to and tried to find a reason mankind would be so cruel to another group of people. That poor little girl, up there for all that time trying to be growing child jammed into that space, never being able to go outside. I was so overcome with emotion people thought I fell and hurt myself.

The museum of the Anne Frank house built a metal staircase to go back down from the upstairs area. A gigantic steel grated staircase for indoor snowstorms.; huge cleats to grab your feet, four feet wide, plenty of senior rump room. That's the ambulance entrance; I'm sure, no gurney would get up that front staircase.

I breezed right down that thing, and you guessed it, just like the Disney World set-up, you dump right into the gift shop.

I bought an Anne Frank diary, a replica of her's, written in German. Why, I don't know? That means, an additional Rosetta Stone CD in German to even begin to read it.

I could frame it and hang the antique ice skates

next to it, only myself would get the meaning of that combination.

I shared my purchase with my husband and once again, he said, "What do you mean you bought it in German?"

That phrase is going on his headstone!

Boarding the Ship, Find the Bar

We toured the City of Amsterdam, floated down the canals, navigated the train system and climbed to the top of the staircase of the Anne Frank house. We saw it all!! Now it was time to get on the longboat and cruise the rivers of Europe.

Our luggage had disappeared from the hotel to the ship, to the stateroom, now if they could continue that service and just carry me to the rest of the sights.

Such a stateroom, floor to ceiling glass patio door, balcony with snow and ice on it, big closet with shelves and cubbyholes for buying things, don't kid me. A nice king bed, suitcases, go under it. Good idea, we usually just open and trip over them. The bathroom has a heated floor, an indication of temperatures to come.

A knock at the door, everything was on a schedule, they just want me to sign how we want to pay for our drinks. Not sure I'm following them, is this a Dutch thing or a cruise thing? I had my choice of paying for each drink, water included or a package. I took the package; I didn't want to sign for every coke I drink, it's a personal thing.

The package was $299, not bad; we are on this boat for three weeks, drinks add up. Back home, the kids easily spend ten dollars a day on mocha, latte, skinny dip, chai, soy coffee's. Over three weeks, that's five hundred dollars! This is a steal; we get the specialty coffees and booze for three hundred dollars!

I was changing clothes for dinner, rinsing my one pair of underwear and drying it with a hairdryer when the PA system went off....

Good Morgan, Good Evening and Velcome to our ship. I thought she was in the room, and I was standing with a hair dryer over my private parts!

Bruce had disappeared; he was out visiting with people he hadn't even met yet. I also learned not to throw open the drapes if the ship is stopped, we could be next to another ship, and that passenger could be drying their underwear with a hair dryer. Not to mention, everyone travels with binoculars.

At another point down the river, I pulled those out to survey the houses along the banks of the river, only to find a pervert in his underwear, looking back at me!

I believed I had my sea legs, after I got everything unpacked and stopped looking out at the moving river. I didn't feel any movement inside, everything I set out on the counters seemed to be staying in place, the toilet water was still; I could join my husband somewhere on that boat.

I'll never understand why he just takes off and leaves me to find him. The longboat is great, sooner or later, he has to turn up, it has one end and then another, unless he jumped overboard to feed those ducks clamoring for bread crumbs, I knew I'd find him somewhere.

He was in the bar, having a house draft beer! I told him I signed us up for the premium drinks package; he didn't have to drink house beer. I grabbed that beer and watered the silk plant at the cocktail table. He just sat there with his mouth hanging open as I ran to the bar and ordered his Crown Royal on the rocks. I was going to get my three hundred dollars worth!

I'm a pathetic drinker; I can't have wine because of the sulfites and my asthma. I don't want hard liquor; the smell reminds me of my Dad's breathe when I was a little kid. I'm not fond of beer; the only thing left is a Shirley Temple, "heavy on the maraschino cherries, please."

I did discover Amaretto on that trip; I could have that on the rocks, slug down two or three, become as obnoxious as anyone else drinking, with no ill effects. It's my new wonder drink. Until the bartender said, I drank all of their supply of it.

"Can't you get some more at the next port," I inquired.

They cater to the wine crowd for re-stocking, so my drinking returned to the Shirley Temples. I told him; he better not run out of maraschino cherries; we were the premium package people!

The bar area was all a modern glass look and more of that frosted milk glass. The bar stools were exotic acrylic pedestals that looked like upside down ice cream scoops. A few drinks in that atmosphere and you are connecting soda straws and drinking from your scoop seat.

That could have been the plan; I never got the meaning behind Danish furniture. There's the Ant chair, the Swan Chair, the Egg chair and the 7 chair; you can count until midnight, but I can't find seven parts to it. Four legs, a seat and back, that's six in American; there is that new math concept, maybe it came from the Danish.

The lecture on the windmills that night at the bar

completely put me in overload. The windmill owners talk to each other by how the blades are directed, on the windmill.

I can tell you I did that in our kitchen with my Henckels set of knives. "Step one step closer to that pineapple upside down cake and I use a meat cleaver on that person." "It is for dessert and it stays there until I put the whipped cream on it!"

As the lecture continued, the event coordinator told us; we would get to tour the inside of real windmill in Holland.

We had to form little groups by a number system and follow a red paddle with that number on it, "All of you 8's come this way!" You had no choice as to who was in the group. The tour guides got together the night before at the bar and decided who would be in each group.

Holy Cow, they had put four, three hundred pound people together to go into the windmill living quarters of about 200 square feet, the other four had to ride the blades!

It wasn't much of a walk to get to the first windmill, with the exception it was raining and snowing at the same time. Two hundred people bundled up and off loaded the boat with umbrellas. We all huddled together and then started the walk to the windmills. The guides were off and running with their little red paddles.

About two minutes into this adventure and one hundred people turned around, headed back to the boat, found the bar, ordered hot buttered rum and took a picture out of the window of the ship. Snow bunny was waving like a crazy women, for everyone to come on back, she found the blizzard to be exhilarating! Her hubby with the red suspenders was glaring at her through the lounge windows.

The event coordinator sent a trainee for that tour; she too stayed behind for the "hot buttered rum"! We were starting to bond, you could tell this was a trip planned by corporate in Miami, Christmas shopping, my eye! We were in the middle of nowhere in Holland, in the winter, can you tell me the travel appeal to that?

I found out later, this weather goes to the Dutch people's heads. They put on swimsuits and dive into the icy waters of the ocean. They chat about the weather for a past time. 'The wind is blowing too hard or too softly, it's too cold or too hot, too wet or too dry... and it's rarely just right. And when it's really hot in summer, they'll say: 'It's either running or standing still, isn't it?' (A Dutch saying).

When a rain shower cools everything down, they will say: 'The good weather never lasts, does it?" And when autumn arrives, they'll say: "Don't you wish it was still summer?" This could explain, talking with the windmill blades, these people made no sense at all!

Grab the Quiet Boxes

The tour guide announced to all of us while handing out the "quiet boxes" for the day, our transmitter radio that she talked to us into earphones. ""This tour includes walks over cobblestones, steps and uneven ground, we recommend you to be in good physical condition to fully participate."

I navigated those steps in the Anne Frank house; I could do this. We were in Koblenz, Germany; I could not miss seeing this castle on the top of the mountain,

There is a movie with Jack Nicholson, and he had a heart attack; his doctor said, "If he could climb a flight of stairs," he could have sex. The uphill climb to this castle was comparable to a straight flight of stairs, ten stories high.

Those of us with asthma, hip replacements and total knee jobs, it was certain permanent disability.

I would go ten feet, stop and gasp for air and ask whoever was nearby to check my pulse, see if I'm alive?

The lovely twenty-year-old tour guide would bounce by us with her cruise ship sign held high and over the transmitter to our quiet boxes she would announce. "Ladies and Gentlemen, not much further, be careful of the uneven rocks and ice!"

Like I cared about rock, I was near death; ice would mean I could slide down the mountain to the warm coffee shop.

Somebody forgot to mention to the guide, the reason this castle had survived eight hundred years of change and turmoil without being significantly blemished, is its location. Not even a pigeon cares to get up that mountain and poop on it, much less cause an enemy attack.

There was a mountain goat on the roof; some people just have to show off!

If there had been a zip line for a walk down, I would have taken it. We did make it back to the ship, and I took the elevator the one floor up to the bar. Don't think I was alone; they were handing out lottery tickets for the three man elevator ride, one floor up.

The bartender thought we were great; we had the premium package. Of the two hundred guests onboard, I think we were the only ones with the premium package.

I thought it was a good deal. And then we met the attorney from Maine. He was drinking by the ticket, as they say, now he is a smart man, he is an attorney. I had to know the reason he did not get the package. Small print...It wasn't a $299 package; it was $299 each person!!!

I did not do well in math in school; I never did master Algebra. I tried to keep Bruce well liquored for the duration of the trip, so that he wouldn't do math either.

That same attorney washed out his own underwear in the bathroom sink and hung it to dry in the room. He packed his own suitcase and took a new pair of boots on the trip. However, he forgot to read the small print, those boots weren't waterproof and he had to put zip lock sandwich bags over his sox's to keep his feet dry! Some people just do not read!

I think people cruise to people watch, and then the gossip gene kicks in and if you find a similar personality to your own, you have your entertainment just by visiting with your cohort.

I hadn't connected with anyone until I met the attorney's wife from Maine. I knew we would be friends for life when she came back from a German village with a box of hair coloring called "Dunkel Blonde." And then proceeded to color her own hair in the bathroom sink. That sink was about the size of a mixing bowl. How she managed to do that is a mystery to me. I suspicion she used the toilet bowl, but I can't prove it and her husband is an attorney. Proof is needed.

After that, we dubbed each other, Frick and Frack. When Frack and I sat together anywhere on board, we were casing out the other passengers.

That couple from West Virginia, he weighed in at 350 pounds and needed suspenders to hold up those poor baggy pants. He had a Barbie Doll wife or companion with him. We called her, "Snow Bunny."

She had at least six different fur hats, coats and boot combinations. Her all white bunny fur hit the ski slopes look, did not blend with his beige trench coat, black knitted beanie hat, he wore all the time. Granted, packing extra coats for a three hundred pound man would take up the whole suitcase. So he traveled light with one outfit, one set of red suspenders and the trench coat.

Over cocktails, Frack and I would contemplate their sex life. Why would she be with him, one encounter and he would suffocate you? It has to be the money for the fur outfits, check out her all blue fox look. And then one day, we saw her up close; she was an old hide from Arizona. Those furs were a distraction; we had other couples to evaluate, on to the Pretzel Woman.

My husband could have a woman come up to him stark naked, and he would continue his conversation on those German coal power plants and not skip a beat. He is missing a male gene. He never gets it when someone is hitting on him, never mind, that I am physically kicking him to make him aware that a woman is hitting on him.

For several evenings, this same skinny woman would make a beeline for the seat next to my husband. He thought she just wanted to talk to him about German coal plants! Frack and I would sit across from them and listen. Bruce didn't hear her say; she had just divorced her third husband. This trip was her re-con mission to get another one, and she had her hooks out for mine. I was sitting right there!

No wonder by the time men are sixty-five, they are divorced three times over. They just don't listen, therefore; they don't see Pretzel woman coming.

This gal settled in and no matter what power plant information Bruce was spewing out, she finished his sentence with, "I teach Yoga." And then, she would curl up into some pretzel configuration and deep breath. He would just continue on in his own little world, talking away, and she was headed for step 2, wrap her legs around her head and convince him she teaches yoga.

That evening the ship had live entertainment, they came in singing and dancing with Pretzel Woman in the front row. Bruce stopped talking to her for the entertainment to begin, my nudging and kicking him was not doing the job.

All of a sudden, this woman takes off her shoes. Flings her legs over the edge of the couch she was contorted in and faces the entertainment group with her feet pointed straight at them. Exposing the largest bunions, I have ever seen.

Frack had just enough wine that this was the topper for her. As soon as the group concluded singing, she turned to me and said. "Frick, you are a nurse, what do they do for BUNIONS?"

She kept pursuing the subject, "I mean Frick, do they cut them off or do they burn them, what do doctors do for BUNIONS?" Pretzel Woman finally got the message.

She plunged those number nines, expanded to fourteens into her dance slippers and shuffled over to another unsuspecting group of husbands.

The Doctors Onboard Are 95 years old!

It is common knowledge, do not go to work sick, do not go on a cruise sick. And then, there are the "suitcase sickies", I call them. They take their germs around the world. Sooner or later their bug will find you. Bruce contracts all illnesses at the one sightseeing spot, I have waited a lifetime to see.

The Louvre in Paris, for instance, I had to rent a wheelchair and push him throughout the entire glass pyramid. He coughed and sneezed, groaned and moaned, with a common cold. There we were in beautiful Wurzburg, Germany about to take a tour bus to the Rothenburg Castle, and he was coughing, sneezing and moaning with another common cold!! I gave him my self- defense kitchen ice pick to traverse the hill, he was on his own.

I think he got it from Pretzel Woman, but what do I know? I made him go, sick or no. I just decided as a retired nurse, I could assess him along the way; there was no ship doctor on the long boat.

We had a pair of retired medical doctors traveling with us. They were a husband and wife team, 95 years old, but hey, they might remember basic cold remedies. However, they couldn't remember what their specialty practice was when they were practicing medicine.

Speaking of them, the little old lady doctor was a real pistol. She had a shuffling walk that could outdo an Olympic runner. And by the clock, she headed out of her stateroom each evening, determined to mark her territory in the lounge for all activities. She left her decrypted little old husband in the dust as she raced for her front row spot. Everyone on board stepped aside for her, we all knew do not mess with her, she documented on her I-pad and held it up to take pictures and shield herself.

She could be up to more than just traveling, don't think they had a home base to return to after the trip. They didn't talk about what might be going on "back home".

Unlike the people from Michigan were always doing; those two fretted about the crock of sauerkraut fermenting in their basement the entire trip. She would look at her husband and insist he tell her how much scum he thought was under the plate of the fermenting cabbage, at home; just before we were putting a fork to our mouth with our green salad.

Or the horse owners who always shared the insemination process, as we were progressing down a buffet line, scooping up mashed potatoes.

In the winter, our fellow passengers were emailing family back home to check on the homestead, the water pipes, the furnace setting, the mail, the newspapers in the, driveway, and if anyone was missing them.

When you think about it, if you are 95, why be in a nursing home? Just book a cruise. Your room is cleaned; sheets changed, and as the oldest passengers, everyone caters to you. You are first in line for food, first in line to tours, first in line to the restroom. Are you kidding me, the 95-year-old doctors figured this out and there was no stopping them.

They didn't climb any hills; they were carried up to the castle tour and returned by chaffer to a warm cafe for coffee and strudel. The rest of us slid off the ice mountain, on our hands, our feet were frozen together. The doctors had breakfast served to them in their stateroom. The rest of us had to be fully dressed, and in line if we wanted a croissant and coffee.

If I was confused on where to go, the staff gave me a map in German. The doctors got electric wheelchairs and escorted to the private entrances of every site they wanted to see. They were never in the crush of humanity, in those Christmas Shops. We never saw them.

They were always back on the ship in the lounge with a sack of fresh hot roasted chestnuts, that some kind soul rushed back to them.

A teenager has this same approach to getting something they want. There's a new secret code for a bag of pot mixed with a dangerous drug in Anesthetics; it's called "Income Tax."

The parent thinks, "Sure go get the forms, learn how to start doing your own income tax." While they are raving how smart their kid wants to advance themselves to a mature level of doing income tax forms, they have just been snowed! "Wow, those forms have gotten expensive, I thought they were free at the post office."

I watched these two doctors "snow" everyone down the river on that cruise.

In a nursing home, no matter how old you are, you have to find your own way to the dining hall. You can stay strapped in a wheelchair with your towel bib on, but your preference of food is whatever strained green or yellow baby food some aid is willing to shovel into your mouth. Your bed is changed once a week. Your room is never clean; it's a once over lightly, empty the diaper pail attempt by housekeeping. If you luck out and get the window half of the room, the drapes are always pulled closed, and you see nothing.

If your family is still around and bother to stop by, it's only once a month, because there is one folding metal chair provided for them. The call bell is on a string, tied to the bedsprings, you have a lottery chance of getting the nurse. They are at the station, eating egg rolls. It is a wise senior who thinks this through and sells everything for a cruising stateroom life.

I will remember this ole gal's approach to old, old, age. I still have the Great Wall in China on the bucket list. If I sell all of my Christmas decorations, we can stay booked on cruise ships indefinitely.

He's Cured, We are in Nuremberg!

The ship docked at Nuremberg; there was an optional tour of the World War II Documentation Centre. Every old man on the ship looked like he had consumed an entire bottle of Geritol, all of his gummy vitamins and a case of that Red Cow energy drink for breakfast. They were all raring to go on this tour!

What is it about war history that bores me into a catatonic state? Ok, Hitler was a bad guy, and we should not forget that, but how many black and white pictures of that crazy dude with the postage stamp mustache can I take in a day?

Our tour guide said, "You have an hour to see 1500 displays and then the bus leaves." We were instructed to check out the large digitally controlled ear wands to self guide us around the museum. We were also reminded to return them to the desk at the end of the tour. The rest of the message was in German, I don't know what she said, she was just pointing to the gift shop.

The hour was up; the others were all re-boarded onto the tour bus. My husband was still deep reading about Hitler and moved at a snail's pace. I told him we had to go. He decided he didn't believe me; he would use alternate plan B. Take a quick look-see if our group were on the bus!

All of a sudden, a siren goes off as if WWII Gestapo squads were coming. An official of the museum was so angry she was turning blue. She kept saying, "You have the vand," but with her accent, it sounded like, "you are a fawn." I grabbed the translator machine. "What is she saying?" Finally, she just looked at him with her loaded gun in hand and said, "Geest geeve it to me!"

These are the moments when I just want to disown him. Find a man weighing in at 350 pounds, with red suspenders and run off to the tobacco farm in West Virginia.

We disembarked the bus, with all the passengers glaring at us! It was below zero with a Gail force wind to walk to the Nazi Rallying Grounds. During the war years, Jews clad in lightweight pajamas were made to quarry and cut stone for this massive outdoor place for Hitler to come a speak once a year! Didn't anyone think to commit the guy? I was bundled up in wool, and fur and layered three deep, with gloves and lined boots. I couldn't cut a pat of butter at lunch following that tour, how those people cut stones is beyond me.

Before we were allowed to eat, we were taken to the Palace of the Justice to see the courtroom where the Nuremberg Trials took place. They chained us together, and pulled us up four flights of stairs, everyone in our group was frozen solid, and we weren't even in pajamas! That history lesson is one I will not forget.

Everything in the courtroom had changed in

appearance from the actual trial day. With the exception of the crystal chandeliers hanging from the ceiling, they were the originals. I had been taking pictures with our digital camera guaranteed to turn out professional quality memories, when the screen read, "memory card out of memory"! How do I convey in German, I left the extra disk in the ship? "

I'm a stupid tourist, I want a picture of this room." "I climbed Mt Everest to see it?" " PLEASE," or "Geest give it to me". I started humming Danke Shon.

Nothing got me a new disk for the camera. I left Nuremberg picture less. A roll of film would not have resulted in this situation. In the dark ages, I took pictures using a camera and a roll of film.

After they were developed, I usually had about three good pictures. The other nine in a roll of twelve were solid black or blurry white; I would have had at least three pictures on that tour. It wouldn't have mattered if the camera did work, in the back of the trial room, in English! "DO NOT REPRODUCE", there are bad vibes in that building!

The chef on the ship had announced the night before; he would prepare an authentic German meal for our lunch, following the Nuremberg tour. Cups of hot Gluhwein were handed to us as we reboarded the ship. I was ready for hot German potato salad and all the trimmings to the German food experience. I changed my clothes in a flash and was first in line to pile my plate high with everything German, whether I knew what it was or not.

Before our trip, I had seventeen thousand dollars worth of dental implant work done. What kind of an idiot would bite down on a brick hard German pretzel? I did, and one of my front implants came flying out and landed under a coffee table.

I tried to be inconspicuous and crawl under that table to find my FRONT tooth. Bruce just kept on talking to some guy and eating. Wouldn't you think he would notice his wife on the floor, crawling around with her lips firmly closed?

Other people did and soon it was an Easter egg hunt of grown adults on the floor hunting for; "What did you say you lost, your contact?, your hearing aid? your pacemaker? "Oh yeah, your tooth?" Bruce finally noticed something was going on, and it involved me.

He could not understand how I managed to break my tooth. I told him; it was not broken just out of place. So being the Mr. fix-it guy he is, he went straight to the ships maintenance engineer, for industrial glue. God knows where that glue had been, but I didn't care at that point,. "Geest give it to me!"

You should know; an implant is half a plastic tooth. I thought I got a whole tooth for $17K. I didn't realize, the implants are designed to last one to three years, at best.

 Three years, if you eat oatmeal, pudding and

strained foods. One year, if you eat your regular diet and one month, if you eat a German pretzel!

My dentist tried to remove that implant tooth after I got back home. He declared that German Industrial glue I used to temporarily fix the tooth would hold until the world ends. Why didn't he use that in the first place? Like a good girl, I returned that glue to the front desk on the ship. I should have kept it for future pop-outs!

The Nurse is Sick

I took extra vitamins, silver hydrofoil, airborne, a B-12 shot, and a Z-pak and I still got his cold!! There is only one approach to a woman being sick, grab a box of Kleenex and forget it! I have traveled thousands of miles, and I will not just go to bed and groan, when there is shopping to do. The Christmas markets were calling; my coat was stuffed with Kleenex, cough drops and a small flask of Crown Royal. If everyone goes cruising sick, then I was going shopping, sick!

In the 1500's, the Germans decided they hated the Jews and banned them from the city of Regensburg. They burned their homes and marched them out of town in four hours. For some unknown reason, they decided to take it a step further, and go to the Jewish cemeteries and pull up the headstones.

They took them back to the village and cemented the headstones into the side of their houses to be a badge of honor that they got those Jews! The tour guide ducked into a courtyard to show us a tombstone embedded into the sidewall of a toilet room. Good grief, I don't know why the Jews don't just go around and kill everyone they see.

This whole tour sounded like our dysfunctional family. "She did this to me in 1990, and I don't forgive her, burn her alive." Or, "forget you, I can have three weddings, and I will never ask you to be my bridesmaid!" I ask these sweet children of mine, "Why can't you just forget the past and move on!" " No, she took my blouse without asking me, and I will never give an inch!" "True, I was twelve at the time, but it is the principle of the thing!" "I'm thirty years old and I have rights!"

At the Christmas markets, you as the tourist think it was all set up to sell their handmade crafts and German clocks. It is a village gathering hole for the locals to drink hot wine and chew on a foot long hard sausage. They could care less about your American dollars; their Euros are worth more, and they know it.

Sick as I was, I still wanted to go in the Cathedral and light a candle and ask God to heal me and get me through the day. I stepped up to light a candle in this dark chapel and fell down into the Bishop's crypt.

Bruce just calmly looked down at me and said, "You do realize, you are in the Bishop's crypt?" "No," I said, "I planned this, just give me a moment to visit here with the Bishop and we can return to the ship." " I'll need crutches, though, see if you can look that word up in the translator machine."

At the end of the day, as the ship pulled away for another town on the Rhine, everyone looked forward to "Happy Hour." At least Frack and I did.

We always dressed for dinner. I brought along enough jewelry to decorate everyone on board. Note to self: If you travel in sub zero temperatures, no one sees anything you have on, much less some necklace under all that grab. I could scale it back.

That night I decided to outdo Snow Bunny. I have a white fur trimmed sweater with rhinestones on it, couple that, with a rhinestone necklace and glass beads and dangle earrings and I was a Christmas ornament to behold.

Frack came in dazzling in a Turquoise sweater with gold dripping jewelry. The other women were glaring at us; they were "relaxing in bulky sweatshirts and sweat pants", they were covering the love handles and letting it all hang out, who were they kidding? People, we will be in Vienna tomorrow, do you not have any good taste?

The know it all woman from Wisconsin reminded us that tomorrow was Melk, not Vienna. This is the woman who is married to the RV parts guy. He likes to monopolize the conversation by going into detail which ratchet he used to screw down the toilets he installed in RVs, thirty years ago.

I mean really, find another dinner table mister. I

cannot stomach his version of RV parts assembly, while I'm dining on my wiener schnitzel.

That woman was a walking encyclopedia and had a mind like a steel trap; she was always right. I had stickies plastered all over our stateroom, to remind us to get dressed, medicated and out the door with a camera.

If it hadn't been for the ships activities director and her PA system announcements every thirty minutes, we wouldn't have made it to any function. But the Wisconsin woman had the written itinerary stuffed in her bra; she was at the ready with more information than the PA system, the Captain, the chef and the owner of the cruise line!

When I am sick, I like hot tea and something sweet. I think my body is infested with a total body yeast infection that requires daily treatments of "something good". It will never go away, and it flares, as they say, during a sick spell.

Each afternoon, the chef had platters of fresh

baked hot chocolate chip cookies placed beside the coffee bar. I begged Bruce from my sick bed to go get me a couple of those hot cookies. I was sure that would perk me up in time for dinner and whatever signature dessert would be coming our way at that time.

He would always return and say, "They are gone, only crumbs on the platter." Something was wrong; anyone I ask about the cookies, always said the same thing. "Oh, I went down to get one and they are always gone". There was a cookie thief on the boat! It was time to hire am attorney!

And then one day, I followed the kitchen staff with the platters of cookies. Who was at the coffee bar, waiting to shove all six dozen fresh baked cookies into her backpack? The Wisconsin woman!! Right is not always right!!!

We had injuries to contend with, our age group has bifocals. The guides can't be responsible for knowing that about us. We have paid extra money to have a progressive, no line bifocals with anti reflective coatings, to look cool and young. Those bifocals are the bane of our existence. Do not push me forward on an escalator; I'm just trying to adjust my eyes to where ever that invisible line is to find a step that coming out at mock one speed. It isn't enough, a ramp can get away from you, or a balcony can be misjudged, in height and width while feeding the ducks, one wrong step can mean life or death if we don't see it!

One night we drew back our sheer drapes to watch the crew ready the boat from the dock and continue on down the Rhine River. They always counted our quiet boxes to see if we were all back on board. However, one couple drank too much and decided to get a breath of fresh air and walk back into town without their quiet boxes.

They were staggering down the dark cobblestone streets when the guy took a flying leap as he tripped on those raised rocks. He landed on his rib cage and shoulder, broke everything possible to break.

A cobblestone street can result in a compound, complex, transverse, oblique, comminuted fracture of the entire body; this poor guy had only one thing going for him, alcohol content of a moonshiners still.

No one was around, and no one heard his wife screaming for help. She drug him back to the dock. The crew began yelling in German to "Wait Captain," while they carried this heap of broken bones, back on board.

The activities director bandaged him in the cheesecloth used for the beer making demonstration. They took him to his stateroom, and we never saw him again.

I think they dumped overboard during the night.

Licorice Whiskey
With The Monks

Buses were waiting for us after breakfast to take us up the mountain to the Benedictine Monastery, for more than 900 years monks have lived in Stift Melk, Germany following the rules of St Benedict. Our guide was dressed as the villagers and had a scarf tied around her head. I thought she was a nun, she had a ruler!

Once she started commanding, I decided she was she was just a local woman with the same "anal retentive disorder as the rest of us." "Don't do this, don't go there, don't touch that and don't take pictures in the library." She had more rules than "Heinz has pickles."

Humm, I'm the one who has spent thousands to come see this Monastery; I'll take a picture if I want to. I'm not going to Hell, if I disobey a control freak.

I just aimed my camera in the library. Wouldn't you know, God was watching me? All of those digitals were of table legs and doorframes, no pictures of the rare books.

The monks at this monastery made whiskey. Not your ordinary whiskey but one that tastes like licorice. A small bottle with a red wax seal on it was 40 Euros. It better be like candy, or this is a fool's paradise. Snow Bunny was buying it by the case. She thought they were cute little bottles of look the same Kentucky Bourbon! She was in for a surprise. When we opened it up, the whiskey smelled like licorice, but it tasted like diesel fuel.

All right, scratch the German strudel; I've had better in Solvang, California. Scratch the Gluhwein, a hot buttered rum tops that! Scratch the rock pretzels, the one's at the county fair back home are hot and soft, no dental repair needed. Now scratch the whiskey. If I want diesel fuel, I will just use a straw and suck it out of the gas tank.

There was a tour of this monastery, the amount of gold and jewels on display for the Bishop robes was staggering. I cannot understand building a hermetically sealed glass case for a solid silver wine challis and then stick the shinbone fragments of some Bishop in it. He should have his own crypt and keep his fragments together.

Taking communion from that cup was never going to happen again. Unless, they use the Monk's licorice whiskey instead of wine, it might sanitize anything.

By the time "crazy guide" pushed us out the back door into the open courtyard, we were ready to stroll down the hill into the quaint village of Melk or where ever we were. Where is that woman from Wisconsin, when you need her? We found a coffee shop and thawed out until time to return to the ship.

It's follow the leader on these cruises. You would think that at the mid-way point of a three-week trip and having shared breakfast, lunch, and dinner with these people, we could find a small cafe and relish in our own coffee and something German. But no, they see you headed somewhere, and the whole gang follows. At that point, you are obligated to give up your prime seat in the window as they are frantically waving in the blizzard, you motion come on in, we'll find a chair for you.

When we got back to the ship, the program director had arranged a talent show from the guests that signed up. I cannot understand people; some woman signed up to read something she had written. SIX PAGES on the function of the brain!!!! Frack and I tried to restrain ourselves; we drank wine and my Amoretto on the rocks to numb ourselves through the ordeal.

There is always one guy in any crowd of people who have no inhibitions left in his mid-sixties. This guy decided to mock her dissertation of the brain with his version of a male strip show. There is no controlling that age group. Those old guys still think they have it with a beer belly hanging over the trousers, barely held up by the red suspenders, their hair dyed sandy red orange, an open shirt with the white hairs, they think they are God's gift to women.

He started gyrating around, yelling out what his brain could do and of course, the ship's crew pulled the curtains off the windows and slid him out of the room to that plank they use to dispose of unruly passengers. Our numbers kept going down; it was the only way to control those old farts.

The next guy on the talent show list decided to sing a love song to his "beautiful" wife. She was, however, recovering from plastic surgery to her face and looked like a black and blue prizefighter. He started out with some love song none of use recognized and ended with Feliz Navidad! The group joined in; it was pathetic. The group got into that one!!

Then we had a professional, Arthur Murray trained guy who brought a paid escort on the trip to dance with him. She was Asian and a stick figure....and they whirled around, intimidating everyone else who might have just shuffled around with their spouse. No guy was going to go up against "Mr. Swing um high and wide" out there performing his tango number. A ship crewmember in training told jokes and sang in the end. It was Academy award winning stuff.

The Blue Danube, Dance with Me

Tell me how the general population of Vienna has a medium income level of about $24,000. When you gaze into the magnificent windows of the shops of Vienna, a sweater is twelve hundred Euros. That's about $1600 American money.

These window displays were of the finest evening clothes for the opera, wools and satins and mens evening clothes. The Italian made Bruno Magli shoes, O.J.'s shoes! That income would support one shoe and one sock at those prices. People are walking around fully dressed, I think there is Target online shopping going on, they can't be buying what is displayed in their shop windows.

Get out the paper map, we had to find the Sacher Hotel and have a piece of the famous Sacher torte. The couple from Wisconsin wanted to come with us. Their fine dining coming from the farm in Wisconsin was Denny's restaurant. I had my reservations as to them doing this excursion.

A Sacher torte is a divine chocolate cake, with raspberry filling and chocolate ganache. It is to be savored and enjoyed with the finest Melange coffee. You must not order a diet coke or a side of fries with it. Never mind, that is exactly what they did. All that the wife of the Wisconsin RV tool man could say was, " I think my German chocolate cake is better than this"....Oh dear, can I get through this?

Time for the Mozart and Strauss Concert....find the people from Maine, Frack will appreciate this. However, the cruise line sets-up these optional excursions and they should see the room they are going to cram three hundred people into, before they book an event.

I was in my finery, fur coat, and all, only to find the room was a sauna. The chairs were hooked to each other, and you were being heated by the body heat of the person next to you. Our programs were worthless hand fans. Times like this call for immediate action, "I will trade my fur coat for that cup of ice you have." "Done, it's yours."

We only had one day in Vienna, and I left my heart there. I shall return, just have to make sure the Wisconsinites are not booked on my next venture. I don't want a quiet box either next time,. I have some body chemistry, and those things quit on me at midday. Along with my feet, my lungs, and my ability to the filter the accent and figure out what the heck they are saying on that machine.

No, next time, we are going first class, and we will take it all in, via private motor coach.

We should go in the fall or spring and be able to see things without the fear of freezing to death, or falling on the ice and being in traction permanently.

That brochure from the cruise ships company was deceiving, " just float down the river and take in Christmas, German style." Humm, their promotion video of the Christmas trip showed blooming tulips in Holland! I didn't connect the dots!

Eighty-Five Locks

I was well into the trip and still didn't know what the locks were? The activities director gave speech after speech on history and I absorbed it about like I did in High School. However, one morning at breakfast, we were sitting next to the floor to ceiling glass windows in the dining room and I turned to look out at the passing scenery, only to see darkness and a wall of cement. I spewed hot coffee all over the waiter, the table and myself, I was terrified, we had sunk and I don't swim. Bruce was no where to be found, he can only go thirty minutes and he is off to the Men's room.

I grabbed my Danish roll and ran to my stateroom. It was darker cement outside the balcony window. I couldn't find the life jacket, and then remembered, you have to be at your "muster station, to get your life jacket."

"Why don't I listen to speeches." I thought it was a condiment station for an afternoon hot dog, not for saving my life. I still couldn't find Bruce and I was hyperventilating by then.

He came sauntering in with his morning cup of coffee in hand, looking perfectly relaxed. I was hysterical, "Quick, grab your coat," I said. " We are sinking," "I don't want you to fade into the water like Leonardo DiCaprio did in Titanic, you need to wear your coat." "I don't know where our muster station is, you've got to help me!"

"Honey," he said. "It's ok, we are going through the locks now". The boat goes down with the water level, we go down, then they let the water in and we go up." There are eighty-four more locks to go," he said.

This wasn't in the advertising video either! "So what do I do, I don't think I want to go through them?" I'll read the handout, they gave at the speech! Ok, it says, "water always flows downhill," well, dah, I do know that! "The lock gates are closed against the pressure of the water." "The lock gates will not open until the water pressure (level) is equal on both sides." Couldn't they just leave the river alone and fish for trout, like we did back home in Colorado? Going up and down in these holes and being trapped in cement for twenty minutes or more is going to take me to Frack's room, and she'll have to "Dunkel Blonde," my white hairs.

It didn't help at the Captains' talk that evening, when he shared, about the loud noise last night. He said, "When we were passing through that lock, I fell asleep and hit the sides, then I had to speed up because another boat was playing tag with me and about to ram us!" He thought that was so funny.

Old red suspenders was hysterically laughing at the Captain. I gave the Captain my mother glare, that if you do that one more time, you are beyond grounded. And I know the kitchen waiter takes him a plate of hot chocolate chip cookies in the afternoon, "you won't get those either, I'm watching you!"

The men on the ship thought going through these locks were the highlight of their trip. They could have saved a lot of money, stayed home and camped out in a tunnel if cement was what they were going for. It just boggles the mind, what excites them.

At the next port, I bought a life jacket and wore it to breakfast from that point forward. I didn't look anymore ridiculous, than Pretzel Woman with her yoga tights on every morning.

Making Strudel, the Right Way

When cruise ships have open water travel time, no ports to stop at, they plan workshops and demonstrations and tours of the boat. Cruising down the river to Budapest took a day and half, so I signed up for the galley tour and hands on to the strudel making demonstration.

The galley on a longboat is about the size of my bedroom closet. If four people can get in there and prepare two hundred dinners, they are miracle workers. I do not believe they can prepare food in that space. I think a speedboat hauls you know what, up the side of the ship about five in the evening and off loads 200 dinners from some local fine dining restaurant. The dinners are all packed in pizza take out boxes in case a passenger happens to see the speedboat.

 It is impossible to plate out two hundred filet mignons, with twice-baked potatoes and broccoli al gratin in a space four foot by four foot. Then finish off the dinner with Baked Alaska! Who are they kidding?

Maybe there was an area off the kitchen with dishes stacked to the ceiling, and they didn't want us to see it, so they just closed off 15,000 square feet. I do that; I throw the dishes in the oven, if the dishwasher is full and someone rings the doorbell.

The chef came out to the lounge area on the ride to Budapest to teach the ladies how to make strudel. The Wisconsin lady popped right up and donned an apron to help him. She makes her own sauerkraut for her grandkids to nibble on when they come visit her. She felt she was experienced in German fare.

He smiled and said "Guten tart, come, help me." She turned and said, "Did he say fart?"

The chef had the dough ready and told her to pull the dough, she insisted on laying it flat and pinching it! Chef put rum soaked raisins and walnuts on top of the dough, our gal, kept saying, "This is not the way I make it."

He kept his cool, although he did yank that apron off of her and served her a bowl of sauerkraut instead of his delicious strudel accompanied by High Tea. It isn't wise to mess with the chef in any country.

Bruce and the guys lined up to see the "Wheel Room". This is a square glass room on top of the boat, that when they go under bridges, collapses down and sends the Captain somewhere below. The guys probably thought they would get a turn guiding the ship down the river, but that day, the thing was a folded deck of cards and the First Mate just pointed to it.

 Not one of those grown men, asked where our Captain might be? They just pulled on their beards and headed back to the bar; they needed to do some heavy thinking on that configuration. It's as if, they will come out of retirement and re-build the ship before we end the trip.

Or, they will dig up Hitler and get him to figure it out! For hating what that guy stood for, I cannot tell you the library of books and tapes and videos we have on him strutting around in bold black and white film. If our cable goes off, on comes the DVD's of Hitler!

That night was the Captains dinner. On river cruises it is not a formal tuxedo occasion, but I still do not know what "Smart Casual" means. Bruce donned his white shirt and tie, but baulked at the dinner jacket. It was minus something degrees outside the whole time we were on that trip, and he is always hot! I'm coming in on the backside of menopause and he is entering it. Perfect for travel.

Smart casual had many interpretations at that dinner. The old doctors were in long evening gown and tuxedo. The Snow Bunny was in a plunging cocktail dress for full view of her recent

40 DDD breast augmentation procedure. The folks from Canada were in cable knit look-a-like sweaters. The pretzel woman was in workout casual tights, no shoes, she still sported the bunions. The Kentucky horse people were in leather. The people from Michigan don't ask?

I came to the conclusion; the cruise line just puts out "Smart Casual", so that the passengers will at least get dressed for dinner each evening. One woman traipsed up and down the corridors in her pajamas, day and night, with her floppy slippers snapping away. Even I know that can't be "Smart Casual!"

Made in China or Budapest

At 11:00 pm, the ship entered the harbor in Budapest. Everything is lit up; it puts Las Vegas to shame. The Presidential palace makes our White House look like a cottage. Everyone on board, with the exception of Frack's husband who went to bed early that night, was outside with a camera, clicking pictures.

Even the 95 year old was out there with her I-pad taking it all in, her husband not to be outdone was shuffling right behind her. At that point, everyone was trying to figure out how to get those two old people back inside before we are holding a memorial service onboard and have to dump them into the icy waters of the River Danube.

And then the sun came up, and the real Budapest came out. We were given a lecture before we got off the boat, "Hang on to your purses, the pickpockets are everywhere." They will take the shoes off your feet; you will never know it until your frozen toes fall off. That wakes you up.

Frack and I discussed over coffee and before we left the ship. Is there anything we need in Budapest? We returned to our staterooms, took off our wedding rings, secured them in our little closet safe, bundled up, and we were ready to shop.

The professional pickpockets know nothing of a woman prepared for an estate sale. We have inner stash pockets to the coat; pre-marked sold stickies, a sharply pointed umbrella for nudging anyone close to our find and a derringer pistol in our underwear. Well, this time, it was in Frack's underwear, I had none.

It was beyond cold, it was arctic that day, both of us ran to the nearest tourist shop and loaded up on wooden stacked dolls, ornaments, and hand knitted forever scarves.

Only to return to the ship and find little gold labels on all of our souvenirs. Reading, "Made in China," affixed to everything we purchased. We had nothing from Budapest, made by real Hungarians. We ditched the labels; those souvenirs became handmade in Budapest, and they were our treasure, who needs to know?

After lunch, we were loaded onto huge buses and took the city tour, however, by this point in the trip, your fellow passengers are now like the next-door neighbors kids to you. You don't like them; you tolerate them. I was tired of forfeiting my front seat for couples with a guy weighing 350 pounds; he can huff and puff his way to the back just like me. It was his choice to eat the entire buffet line, the bus tour is not nap time, snore time, pass gas time; I came here to see something!

It was a blizzard out there; my fingernail file served as the window scraper. And didn't they say, this was a Mercedes Benz bus? I think we have the chicken bus again!

There was no heat; the RV part's guy was disassembling the air conditioner unit overhead, trying to find the heater. The driver was turning blue, yelling in Hungarian. The tour guide had earphones on and was rocking out. She had char truss pink hair, and a mini skirt over tights, with leather biker's jacket, some rhinestone jewelry punctured all over her face, lips and ears. She didn't seem to want to get involved; she did connect her music to the PA system, and we all lost it.

That night at dinner, we all sat and just looked at each other. No conversation, just eating the game hen and truffles in silence. The appetizer was a hot cup of pea soup with a swirled froth on it, no one even commented on pea soup in a glass cup; they just drank it down. It was that point of no return; we were done, vacationed out and paralyzed.

All of a sudden, local entertainment came on board. Dancing fairies, maybe cross-dressers, flying across the room with chiffon flowing everywhere! How did they know, just what this crowd needed? Maybe 180 people excused themselves to their staterooms to take evening medication, and watched a repeat of N.C.I.S. With a drink to go and dessert on a plate, we all stood in unison and left the ballerinas to float about the bar area.

They were delighting Pretzel Woman!

Prague and Goodbye

It was time to get off the ship and say goodbye to our river cruising family. First though, the last casing of the room, the final walk-through, don't forget Bruce! I could not forget my wedding ring in the little room safe and the prepared gratuity envelope. It was still sealed. Those envelopes are paper piggy banks; I'm known to rob at will.

People were hugging the housekeeper, the bartender, the pianist, the chef, and the activities director. I found the maintenance engineer; he did get the tooth back into my mouth. They were stuffing money into the staff's hands, coat pockets, shoes, whatever; money was flowing everywhere.

No one seemed to notice, the ninety-five year olds. They shuffled out onto the disembark ramp and got themselves loaded into the bus for the airport while all of that mushy money exchange was going on.

And that tells you why they can live on the ships and travel the world. Just save the gratuity money up, and you have your next cruise booked. What we gain in wisdom, in old age...

Bruce and I stayed another three days in Prague. Extensions to trips are fantasy at home before the trip, "As long as we are there, let's stay another three days!"

At the end of three weeks, I was exhausted trying to be a tourist. I envied the majority that took the "A" bus and headed for the airport and home.

I would have agreed to be tied to the tail of the airplane. I had a Budapest hand knit scarf; it could have served as a hammock, I would have been as comfortable as First class. I would have provided my own drink service.

If you are in the middle section of the plane, by the time your little cup of drink reaches you, you have about a thimble in liquid left to drink. My alternate plan, (I have them too!) I didn't need a seat, I would stow away in the bathroom, I could lock it and stay in there, perfectly comfortable compared to my paid seat.

Ten couples, including us, decided to extend the trip three days in Prague, in the dead of winter. Now we were with the nine other couples which we had the least contact with the whole time.

The bane of my existence, Wisconsin Women, the RV part's guy, the Canadian book worms, the Pretzel Woman, West Virginia tobacco man. Oh dear God, how will I do this?

Those extension days were not organized; we were on our own. I missed the PA system telling me what to do. We couldn't even find our hotel room, and we were bussed up to the door. It was an atrium lobby with huge trees growing in it and plants everywhere, the rooms were somewhere above the foliage, but we couldn't find the elevators.

The extension pamphlet said, "Our cruise line people will be at the hotel to help you check-in." A clerk, who speaks fluent Czechoslovakian with a handbook in English, can at most get me to the bathroom!

The only logical thing to do was have Bruce climb a tree and scope out the surroundings. He was not receptive to that approach in finding our room.

By the end of the trip, he had perfected a new strap on method to the luggage, and he looked like a walking luggage rack. He had purpose; he's always trying to perfect somebody else's trade. That guy who helps you with his luggage, that's his living! Just give in and let him do it, your strap method is a chiropractor's dream come true. I carried Dilaudid somewhere in my purse!

The only thing left to do, follow Wisconsin woman, she found the stairs! The West Virginia tobacco farmer was waddling down the corridor, snapping his suspenders; he took the freight elevator! Oh sure, like I'm going to stoop to that!

Prague is a giant ashtray! Everyone including infant's smoke! I cannot shop effectively in a cloud of smoke; it was worse than the marijuana in Amsterdam. The Czech cigarettes are smuggled into the county from Poland or Ukraine, through an underground tunnel, dropped on the railroad track and the cows must tramp over them before they reach the border. They smell to high heaven; a gas mask couldn't filter those things.

The young people in Prague are making a fashion statement to take up the electric cigarette. Those plastic puffers must be dipped in formaldehyde, most of those girls looked like my souvenir prune dolls from Germany.

We take for granted; our country has come a long ways in tobacco education; our kids are putting Fentanyl patches on and then smoking pot. They won't shrink; they just fall down and don't get up!

The West Virginia tobacco farmer was again popping his red suspenders and picking up real estate information; you could see the dollar signs in his eyes. Another kill zone!

Did We Just Buy A House?

My mind was acting like the GPS lady in the car, a constant "re-calculating". I woke up in a hotel in Prague and needed to go downstairs to the breakfast buffet and pay the dining bill! Cruising puts you in another world; it's all pre-paid, I did not want a dining ticket, I can't calculate the Korn.

And then, there we were again, having breakfast next to the man and his Asian wife from the ship. She never stopped talking and complained about everything she ate. She ate all Asian foods and continued to complain about that "German crap food" from the trip!

Now what possessed them to take a European holiday trip, if she only wanted sushi? Then too, he may have planned the trip, turned off his hearing aids and wanted some meat and potatoes. He smiled most the time; he may have gotten his way.

Manipulation is at the heart of every marriage; you could just tell he knew how to get around her..."Ok honey, we'll go to a Vietnamese grocery store, buy what you want." " I'll take a quick run for a Big Mac. "Dang, I sprained my ankle." "You'll need to load that stuff into the house!"

How about the senior husbands at the drugstore, loading the booze onto the rolling belt by the gallons. They may even have coupons in hand, but they are willing to run that ticket up into the hundreds for their "Royal Crown." And then, their wife follows with a magazine and a candy bar and he goes ballistic, she's spending money! She shrinks away and he whistles at her! She unwraps the candy bar, and starts barking like a dog! Marriage manipulation!

The couple from Canada were always the early birds in the dining room on the ship. Here they were again, half way through breakfast when I didn't even have control of my bra hooks.

They took to the streets early; I kept buttering my

toast and checking the streets, with a glance at the morning blizzard. What could she possible want out there? What did they think they were going to see? They were dressed in black; taxis can see a black blur coming down the street, white is sure death.

That Canadian lady always had a lovely felt hat on with the expensive feather standing straight up from the brim. She got a rude awaking in Prague. It rained and snowed together all day, she returned to the hotel with a limp bone feather connected to that rain soaked hat. Her dapper look turned into wilted lettuce every day.

Her husband bought her a 1200 Euro sweater in the window in Vienna and the signature wool hats at 400 Euros each. She had back up.

Pretzel woman was still with us, but on her own to find that Hungarian new guy. She was in the bar lounge each evening, contorted into some Yoga position trying to reel one in. I don't know what the outcome was; I just had to think, if you keep those feet out there with those bunions in full view, do you think, some guy is finding that exciting? You could be playing footsie and be seriously injured with those protrusions!

And, you guessed it. The Wisconsinites!! Who now wanted to have Christmas Eve dinner with us. There was only one thing to do; sell my diamond ring and book the two million five hundred thousand Korn Christmas Eve dinner in the fine dining room!

That did it; too expensive for their blood. They walked four blocks down the street to get a 50 Korn sausage and sauerkraut buffet, all you can eat. She called the grandkids, saying, "Guess what Gramm's eating, your favorite snack, sauerkraut!" We're bringing you some……

Christmas Eve in a foreign country meant no tree for us. The hotel strung some twinkle lights on the atrium trees. Bruce had more tangled in one box, in our basement, than that. The emotions were welling.

They were serving sauerkraut soup for Christmas Eve to see the "piglet", what piglet? Is that a significant souvenir? I have wooden dolls stacked together with a surprise bean in the last one. I have a carved rock of sandstone; it should have been a garnet, but those korns scare me. I have a puppet, his face wasn't happy, a mismade defective one: but then I wasn't happy when I bought him, we bonded. But a piglet, I just didn't know how to pack a piglet!

The locals had a live Carp floating in their bathtubs for Christmas dinner, the next day. I asked the waiter to explain that one to me. He said, "They put the Carp in a bathtub of cold water." "Is the tub clean? Or does the fish care? Do they kill it in the tub, or add bubble bath?

I'm going to eat my turkey next year in full cowboy attire; I need to be home, I need to thank my ancestors for my turkey.

I didn't bow my head in thanks for sauerkraut and

carp; I bowed my head to think about turkey, and dressing and mashed potatoes. Bruce poked me to come up for air; people were looking at me. Why, I didn't have my rear end up in the air?

We were at the end of the fabulous European Holiday cruise, and something happens to the body. A weary gene marches out and states very clearly; I don't care what magnificent palace we've paid five hundred dollars to see; I don't care who is buried where, I don't care about anything except a warm bed, and thermal socks, this has got to end!

I gave Bruce an ultimatum, I thought of flat Stanley. Could I cut out a cardboard image of myself and you hang my camera around its neck, drag me down the rain, ice slick streets and say I was there! I'll wait in the hotel, what do you think?

The next day, we followed that fourteen-year-old tour guide to the Lebowski Palace. We were to walk to the palace; it was to take an hour. The guide kept saying, "we're almost there." He got lost, and that one-hour promise turned into three hours. Remember Gilligan's Island, same thing, only below zero, arctic conditions?

We paraded through this magnificent palace, like a bunch of herded sheep. This is a money raiser for this already incredibly wealthy family. Their youngest son tripped off to university and came back with a bright idea. Let's parade the American's through the palace, charge them an outrageous entrance, feed them some goulash and nail them at the gift shop on the way out!

We finally made it to the included lunch, in the family quarters. I was expecting a buffet of hot Hungarian delights. It was a small finger bowl of goulash, no bread and a glass of cold water. I asked the waiter, "Can I have a cup of hot tea?" "No," he replied. It is served with the cheesecake at the end of the meal. He would not budge, no hot tea, until dessert was served. "Eat your goulash and drink your water. Hagyj békén!" (Leave me alone, crazy woman!)

If I win the lottery, I'm buying the Hearst Castle in California. I'll put together the same package; see if I can get the Hungarians to come over for my tour. I'll have them walk up the road to the Castle, take the tour, end up in the wine cellar, serve them some apple cider, some cheese and crackers, maybe bring in some fish tacos! The gift shop would be the passage out; they would need to buy perishable guacamole at $125.00 an ounce.

So it was back to economy seats in the airplane home. I managed to get four hundred pounds of souvenirs through customs at the reduced rate of an extra hundred bucks. That makes the gingerbread ornaments price out to five dollars instead of fifty cents, and the Budapest (made in China) bobbles, at three times their value, but I have my memories of the Christmas cruise.

After eleven hours on a plane to Miami, we piled our luggage on the cart and faced the music. The dreaded line to CUSTOMS!

How can 5000 people in twenty cattle guard lines, be processed by three officials? Who set that up?

They have two guards with machine guns and several crotch-sniffing dogs ready for middle age women who want to speak to a supervisor. Can't be done, wait it out.

Pretzel woman cut in front of me; I had to implore my estate sales tactics, I used my umbrella tip and stomped on her bunions!! We were finally home!

Head North Young Man or Old Man

As we traveled about the United States, my husband decided at one point; he wanted to take a position in Minneapolis, Minnesota. Mind you, we were in the South, when he exists left, and heads for Minnesota. He has one medication that causes confusion; I need to check on that!

Whenever I watched the national weather reports through the years, Minnesota always came up with the lowest temperature on record. I never heard about those people up there; I never saw stories of tourism in Minnesota. I did know they had ten thousand lakes, but does anyone live by the lakes? Or, is it all frozen tundra twelve months of the year?

These are the questions for a person moving to Minnesota, and then it became crystal clear to me. The Mall of America!! That would be the call of the north...I cannot turn down a mall. That is the largest mall in the nation; I will go!

But first, we needed to unpack the RV and re-pack into the travel trailer (my walk-in closet). I watched my husband unload, re-arrange and re-load that walk-in closet in dismay. He always seemed to chose the hottest day in the south to attempt his organizational re-do. Which would give him about thirty minutes maximum; to enter, unload, become completely dehydrated and collapse.

Then his mood changed, he would become a drill sergeant and bark out his commands according to whatever was frustrating him the most. The boxes were too heavy, or too large, or too small, too cheap, too expensive or any of mine, not necessary. His giant toolbox mega-chests were completely necessary for road travel.

It had been a cold day in July, since he had a woodworking project going to utilize that router of his. Never you mind, he was not parting with one of those fifty screwdrivers, twenty odd drills or box of hammers, must less that router. All were absolutely necessary.

He took a different approach to the distribution of weight this time, I thought it had a teeter-totter effect to it; all the heavy items were up front, the back was open space.

I don't have a physics degree, but I wondered about that look. He mumbled something to the effect of "needs to be over the axle." You reach a point in a marriage after almost forty years, if something does not work; don't blame me, I gave you the look. He knows; that look has been more often right than wrong. But what do I know?

So the move to the great land of the lakes began. We put the recreational vehicle on an RV sales lot. We called for a transporter to haul that walk-in closet up north. He winterized the car for the journey, no, he didn't, he just said, he was "going to winterize it"! It's a known fact; motor oil freezes at -40 degrees. My weather app said, it was

-40 and a Polar Vortex in Minnesota. Wonder if there is an app telling us how to remove frozen motor oil, I'll take my kitchen ice pick!

The transporter arrived on time the morning of departure with a coffee cup in hand. Time is money, he was raring to go, I escorted him to the trailer to hook-up and some good ole boy had parked his pick-up right in front of the hitch! Who does that? Who belongs to the pick-up, where is the park manager? This is a problem. In days of yesteryear, you could put that truck in neutral and give it a push. Not so much now, it had a digitally controlled panel to open the door, automatic transmission and steering wheel bar lock on it! That puppy wasn't going anywhere.

The manager of the RV Park had his girlfriend live in the house at the park; he lived in the woods somewhere. She called him by ham radio or coded leather straps in the tree trunks. I heard this over and out exchange and then she returned to tell me. She said, "That guy's girlfriend is going to come unlock his truck for you." I thought all

Southerner's were married; it just looks that way; they are slow at everything, slow to commit.

That woman came careening into the park, with her coffee cup in one hand and cell phone in the other. She was steering with her knee and pulled in next to that truck. She jumped out; cell phone still attached to her ear and punched in that digital code to the truck door. She slid into the seat and backed that truck out of the way, hollering, "He does this all the time." The transporter hooked up in record time, took a look at the trailer, scratched his head, and was on his way.

About five hours later, I got a call from my husband who was now setting up his office in Minnesota and waiting for me to "tie up the loose endings" and get there. His voice was frantic; it's always frantic, if he drops the tone and speaks slowly.

"We have a problem," he said. "The transporter had all four tires on the trailer blow out, too much weight!" "Really," I said. He quickly followed that with, "He has put all new tires on and needs to offload the weight." "OFF LOAD, what does that mean?" "It means; he will take out half the stuff, yours really, my tools are too heavy, and he will put your stuff in a storage locker, in a dirt field, somewhere in North Carolina."

And then, in the same breathe, he added, "You need to drive there and give him the key to the trailer." "What?" "How far away is he?" "Three hundred miles, he's waiting for you."

There are no lampposts on the back roads of South Carolina. When the sun goes down, your headlights reflect off the red eyes of deer, and that is it! We always have a charger in the car connected somewhere under the seat and in a secret compartment. I grabbed my cell phone, my purse, stopped for gas and was on the road to find the dirt storage locker and "OFF LOAD!"

My girlfriend in Maine is a retired schoolteacher. She taught her third grader's all of the nation states and their capitals; using a vinyl dinner table placemat, shaped like the United States. I bought one. I cannot read a map in the car, or follow GPS or route in my phone, I become car sick. But a quick glance at the US placemat and I'm good to go, back on track.

It wasn't working that evening driving the back roads to try and find this dirt field the trailer was supposed to be waiting for me. Again, grab the phone and set the GPS. The power was at 14%! The only thing to do was pull off the side of the road, break my momentum, but I had to charge the phone. My non-sharing husband took the charger to Minnesota! Now what?

I'm dead in the water; I had pulled into a swamp! Southerners close up shop at all stores, gas stations and homes at about five in the evening. I didn't know where they go but it was dark, and there was no one out there on that road, except me, the deer, and whatever lurks in the swamp water.

After a three-hour drive, I found the storage lot,

and there was the transporter, another cup of coffee in hand. He broke the lock and had it all off loaded and was raring to go again! "So you don't need the key," I asked. "How do I get back to the RV?" "Is there a Ritz Carlton out here somewhere, I'm not handling this well?"

Another lesson in technology, if you are without your charger plugged into the car, you can take the charger by your bed, connect a USB plug to it and transfer that to the car....REALLY. I'll get that tattooed on my upper thigh for future reference.

Following the placemat map, you leave South Carolina, go through North Carolina, head over to Kentucky, and then angle through Illinois, Wisconsin and into Minnesota. Or follow GPS and go to Virginia, Pennsylvanian, and NY, then ferry across the Great Lakes. Eventually, you get there.

The Five-Year Storage Locker

When we made the decision to see the USA in our RV, not the Chevrolet! We packed up all of our worldly goods and houseful of furniture and put it all into long term storage. We chose a locker facility with a live-in resident manager; air-conditioned space, an outside roll up door for easy access to a moving van and in Las Vegas.

That way, when we checked on its condition periodically, it would be a fun trip also. Take in a show on the strip and hit the slots. In the five years our home was in storage, we never went back. I called the office periodically, the resident managers came and went, sometimes they answered with, "Who and what number did you say?" Elvis isn't there anymore, why go?

Now that we were in Minnesota and unable to live in a recreational vehicle at forty below zero, it was time to go get the household goods in Las Vegas.

The moving van would meet me at the locker, and I would have my things again. I booked a flight and then realized the fun trip was not going to be, I had to be at the storage facility at 7:00 AM, find it on the vinyl place mat and be on the return flight, the same day.

I had one night stay close to the storage facility at the "Come stay with Us Motel" at the end of the Strip. No breakfast included no towels, instant coffee, pay for the toilet by coin. I would have done better to sleep in the rental car; at least I would have had the GPS lady for company.

What they do not tell you about long-term storage is that if you don't hermetically seal the door to the unit, your belongings will be covered with six inches of thick desert sand. Nothing will resemble what you once had. Everything was haze grey, including me to board the airplane. How do you explain that to the person sitting next to you on the plane, that you are not a street bum from Vegas, who must have won a jackpot?

Minnesota in the fall is very beautiful, the fall colors on the trees, people hiking, biking, bicycle riding, smiling and in shorts at forty degrees. They are a hearty bunch. We, however, were in parkas, gloves, and hats and clung to the hand warmers in the pockets of our coats.

The weather forecast said snow was coming, so I thought maybe we should decorate the outside of the house for Christmas before it was too cold to hold a string of lights. Good thought, other neighbors, were doing the same thing. In California, our house was the talk of the neighborhood with the Christmas light display. After all, Dad worked in electricity or something like that, none of us really knew for sure. "Light up the house for the kids," was his motto.

This Minnesota neighborhood we were in was made up of young families in their thirties, no seniors to be found. One house was closed up and empty; they were in Florida! Bruce felt he needed to show these young folks how a Christmas light display is done. He bundled up, waved to a neighbor in his shorts and started untangling the outdoor lights.

After all these years, you would think he would ascribe to putting them away in some order so that the next year would be easier to put the lights up. He was out there tugging, pulling, mumbling and doing his own thing for hours. I ventured out occasionally and handed him a cup of hot tea, then hot bourbon, then ask if he wanted me to start an IV; I couldn't stand the cold to keep coming out. He never sees the humor in life!!

Back to the Christmas lights, he covered all the bushes with colored lights and one spindly little tree in the front yard he threw lights on as high as he could lasso them up in the thin branches. Then he hung some blinking plastic snowflakes on branches that were sagging. He circled the flowerbed around the spindly tree with colored lights that blink on and off as if they were running down a track. It was a Las Vegas event!

The neighbors hung their clear icicle lights on the

eaves of their houses, waved goodbye as they returned to their cozy fires. Bruce kept on tweaking and finished with his crème de la crème, he synchronized the lights to a music system staked into the grass. He turned the volume up as if the wild birds might enjoy the repeating sound of "You better watch out, Santa's coming to town" in the air!

And then it snowed, and snowed and snowed. The temperature kept dropping and the snow became ice. His lights in the bushes were mere blurs of color under the snow, his trailing Las Vegas event show was under snow and the music was muffled. The neighbor's lights on the eaves of their house shone brightly.

Apparently no one removes the decorations encrusted in the ice until spring. They might hack them out when the annual ice-fishing contest happens. It's a Minnesota mystery as to when the Christmas decorations come off the house, or it is a side business to the snowplow man, and he just crushes them. Start new the next year!

That next March, on St Patrick's day, his music box hidden in the frozen snow was still paying Silent Night! We didn't get invited to any Christmas get-to-gathers on the cul-de-sac, could have been they regard Californians as somewhat weird and wanted to keep their distance.

Things improved when I insisted he wipe off the snow and ice to the license plates showing South Dakota.

The Mall of America

Everyone I know has been there; I was going to go to that mall. I had one problem, well, maybe two problems. Surgery on my knee two years ago for a torn meniscus had never healed right. There is a pocket of fluid below the knee that resents any walking for longer than ten minutes. It swells up like a tennis ball and is only relieved if I sit down and talk to it. And then about three months before the move to Minnesota I had a rotator cuff repair surgery to my shoulder.

I was instructed not to lift any more than five pounds. I cannot go shopping without my purse. My purse weighs in at least twenty-five pounds. This trip to the Mall of America had to have some special provisions put into place. Empty the purse; cull it down to the bare essentials. Check the credit card status and move the entire credit limit over to one card! THINK SMALL, THINK SMART, think Ninja shopper!

Every shopping center has a customer service counter. If you relinquish your driver's license, some cash, your birth certificate, your passport and a free and clear title to your home, you can rent a wheelchair to see the mall and shop until the person pushing you drops.

Bruce agreed to get a wheelchair for me and off we went. He would not agree to the locker for your coats, hats, gloves and snow boots. Those he piled in my lap and was so pleased he had saved two dollars! I, on the other hand was straining to see over that pile as we explored this huge structure.

About an hour into the experience, he had to take me to the infirmary my core body temperature was about 105.0 degrees! A sweet physicians assistant shook her head and said, "You need to get a locker Sir, and you are suffocating her."

In the middle of the Mall of America is an amusement park, with a roller coaster and huge rides swinging overhead. They built the ground up like hills and covered it with rocks and slides and all fun rides for kids.

Bruce started pushing me through it to get me to the other side of the amusement parks, his breathing pattern changed; he huffed and puffed and finally let the wheelchair go, and I was on my own. The only thing that stopped me was the pile of coats, hats and gloves in my lap as I hit the exit to the seven acres of wild rides. Now he had a second reason for not checking those into a locker, they were auto buffers.

People get so upset with a wheelchair. Grandma in the wheelchair has as many rights as the drooling toddler in the killer stroller. Those three wheel strollers can run over a foot, run up the back of the leg and disable a person in one fell swoop.

The center of this park is like an Arizona Roundabout. I gave that concept to Arizona, because heat can fry the brain. There is no sense to everyone coming to the same spot and vying for the same spot! Human nature will take over, and it becomes a "round dee round." Everyone is driving in circles; no one getting anywhere and fear of loss of life or limb looms, as they all converge in the middle.

An architect planned this Roundabout concept for the mall. Are they nuts? Kids running at mock one speed, Dad's pushing strollers loaded with coats and packages; Mom's carrying the babies in those slings at mock two speed all converging for the same center spot. And where is Grandma in the wheelchair? In the middle, helpless, in the chair, covered with coats, and then what happens? Grandpa has to pee, and he's gone!

After about six hours in the Mall of America, you progress to the top floor of restaurants and theaters. Another six hours, you must leave; your rental is up, and you will not get a passport, birth certificate or drivers license back if you do not return that wheelchair in time.

There are luxury hotels next to the Mall of America. I believe a good number of seniors crawl out the side door of the mall, make it to the lobby of the hotel and check in with the one memorized credit card number left in their head. No sense in memorizing your social security number anymore, call your dentist or pet shop, they have it on file. But credit card number, that is essential.

The locals don't go to the Mall of America; they say it's too big! So who goes? The Minneapolis airport has a runway full of planes lined up to be sprayed with pink de-icing foam, those folks are on they're way out. No planes coming inbound with tourists wanting to shop, that runway is six foot deep in snow.

So who is shopping? I maintain the people stuck in the Roundabouts. Canadians may be coming down to warm up!

The Lobster Race

The day you finish putting away all the Christmas decorations, clean up the glitter on the floors and dig the ornament hooks out of the carpet, your socks and the vacuum cleaner; is the day, you are too tired to bake those forty dozen cookies.

The kids are grown and gone; there is one package under the tree, and that is from all of your kids. It was a lonely, bare, over-decorated house with two people trying to keep up the traditions; it was time to take the party somewhere else.

Spontaneity occurred with the click of the cursor. We booked a flight and in the middle of the night, when all of the children are tucked in, and Santa is filling the room with delights across the nation, we were flying to Maine to see our friends from the River Cruise.

Flying First class on Christmas Day, means no shoes have to be pulled off, you can leave your belt on, if you want a wheelchairs, Santa will push you? Hey, I took it all and bring me a hot coffee, Kahlua with cream. However, if they can waive these TSA musts on Christmas Day, do they ever consider a terrorist might figure that out?

Maine gets ice storms, and they had just had one when we rented a car at the airport to go on to Boothbay where our friends live. As we were slipping and sliding along the snow packed highway, knowing full well 10,000 people had no electricity this Christmas morning, I still thought the trees looked like Waterford Crystal, and I wanted to break off limbs and take some home. That would be, as close to a Waterford collection, I would ever get. All Bruce could say, is" Ice melts dear." Why is he always right?

Frack and Mike are the Mainer's from our River Cruise trip that we bonded with and will now stay friends, until death or complete senility, and we don't recognize one another. Which ever comes first.

Frack was so excited that we were coming that she had monogrammed stockings on the fireplace for us too. I decided to one up that one and dress Bruce in a Santa suit, complete with white dyed eyebrows and icicles off his nose. He got out of the car, grabbed his big bag of Santa gifts and together with me in a red wool coat, white fur hat and a fur muff, we made our grand entrance. No kid in the mall was as excited as Frack; of course what she wanted was my muff. We looked at each other and said at the same time," I've always wanted a muff! " A few tears, we were good to go.

Christmas dinner in Maine, it's a given, LOBSTER. And lobster we had, but first, live lobster races on their kitchen wood floor. Even though those eight, two-pound lobsters had just been pulled from the icy waters of the sea that morning, they all looked drunk.

A lobster knows; he is confined by giant rubber bands, something is about to happen. His only recourse is to poop on the floor. That does not stop the dunking squad to their demise; they are headed for the hot tub. The only humane thing to do is soften the blow with a bed of seaweed in the bottom of the pot, keep the lid on and don't look back!

Frack set up the first race. I never win anything, and my lobsters just stayed put and dug their little extra legs in, continued to poop and gave me a sign with their antennas similar to those on the highway with road rage.

I don't know who won the race; they all got their fifteen minutes of steam reactor explosion, turning them into cherry red delicacies. I can't form an attachment to them; they are too good to eat, Maine good and only 90 calories, I never factor the butter. Does an Eskimo count the calories of seal oil? No, they need it for survival. After the ice storm, that was survival food.

Let a Mainer teach you how to eat a lobster, it is better that any dissecting science class you've ever had. First, put your hooded sweatshirt on and roll up the sleeves, it was going to get sloppy, messy.

Take hold of that creature and start pulling, pull it all apart, don't be concerned with all the liquid frothing forward, that lobster had a reserve tank.

Grab the crusher claw. Well, I would if I knew where it was. The Mainer will fill you in on what that is,. It can be right or left, the lobster couldn't make up its mind, so it hardened one up for you, that's it!

Now roll you're "bug" as lobstermen call these salt-water cockroaches! OMG, I've always thought they looked like a cockroach and now you want me to enjoy this thing? Unfurl the tail, and with one twist, break it away from the bug's body. Try not to think about any of it, just dip it in drawn butter and get on with it.

And then the Mainer will going to talk about the "green stuff", that slimy goop is supposed to be a liver, however, no anatomy dissecting class I ever attended had a liver that disgusting. It serves the same purpose as man's liver; it filters mercury and contaminants. Why would somebody think that was a delicacy?

The class continues as to whether this is male or female, those red eggs, the "Roe"; that's a delicacy too. God, I hope the mortician doesn't think that way with me! Mine, if any left are old and rubbery, it would not be a delicacy.

By the time they get to the scrawny little legs they want you to suck on as a straw, my appetite is ruined. I'll take mine pre-picked, poked and yanked with just a tail to deal with, served on a platter and a Key Lime tini, heavy on the sugar rim.

High Centered on the Ice Cap

We baby boomer's all think the same if we have guests come visit us. No matter the weather condition, we feel the need to take them on the grand tour of our part of the country. I had been to visit my friend Frack once before in Maine, in the dead of winter, and our catch-up talking got us into some tense moments on that visit.

She forgot to stop for gas, and as we were seeing the backcountry, she happened to notice the fuel gauge. I thought she handled it well, although in retrospect, I now know she was faking it. She turned somewhat pale and said, "I don't want to alarm you, but we are a little low on gas." "How low?" I responded. We hadn't seen a single car for miles, and it was freezing cold. "Ohhh, pretty low," she said, "Past the red line?" She nodded, yes.

"Oh dear, I'll have to read the manual now, I get

nauseated reading in a car." "Don't light up a cigar, that will cause me to up- chuck." "The manual says fourteen miles to the gallon, do you think we have a gallon?" " I don't know," she said. I then told her," We have to suck out the remaining gas with a soda straw and measure it, or coast the car from here on out." Frack chose coasting. When we found the one gas station within fifty miles of anywhere, we coasted right in there and kept right on talking.

This trip, Mike wanted to show Bruce their summer lake cabin. We all bundled up and headed for the lake, after a nice beer and lobster roll stop at the pub. The road to the cabin gets plowed every week or so, seemed harmless. Although no one lives at the lake in the winter, it is frozen over, power is sporadic and the woodpile is frozen unto itself. The snow was about two feet deep as we approached the cabin and had a hard frozen top crust.

Mike found a set of tire tracks and pulled off into the tracks. There was an odd crunch sound when he shut off the engine. The river boat on the Rhine made that sound when it banged into a frozen lock; however, the Captain said, "Don't worry. I forgot to adjust the steering!" "Isn't that what the Captain of the Titanic said, "No worries, this is normal for this time of year." Mike thought it was normal, Frack seemed ok, I just have crunch paranoia.

Man rarely pays any attention to car sounds or house sounds. Bruce usually says, "What you mean a funny sound?" So, I have learned not say, "Did you hear that?" Because first of all, he will say that famous phrase; and secondly, he probably didn't hear me ask the question anyway.

I was thinking these two guys have similar traits; we would just see what that crunch meant after we hiked to the cabin. The car could be on the lake, and it would have sunk by then.

Old hard topped snow should be like walking on a hardwood floor. I lived in snow country fifty years ago; I'll give it a go. I forgot; you are on top of the hard snow for about thirty seconds, then your foot plunges down into the two feet to four feet of snow. You then lose your balance, and you are at that point, a snow angel! What people our age have to come to terms with is, I had just had shoulder surgery, those screws in there were now somewhere in the snow.

When we returned to the car, the sun was going down, and we were ready to go back and find a nice glass of wine and nibble on those hors d'oeuvres, Frack had stashed away. Mike started up the engine, and all four tires spun in unison and free from the ground. We were high-centered!

Bruce jumped out of the car to dig the snow out. Locals usually do not have survival equipment in their cars, the Mainers, for sure. They just look at the situation and say, "Ahhh, yup, It's up on a pile of snow and ice."

No shovel in the trunk, no shovel in the shed, it, was locked for the season. Bruce went into Boy Scout mode, when he was never a boy scout. Mike was the Eagle Scout! Maybe Bruce was in his native Los Angeles mode; steal from the neighbors, run like hell.

He promptly took a shovel off of somebody's porch. They dug and dug and cussed and dug. And then they started huffing and puffing, time to call the emergency road service.

Frack would do that; she was poised with her cell phone like a six-gun. That woman became a new person over the phone. "What do you mean, you can't find us on your GPS?" " I have been a customer since the 1800s!" "Geest get here!" she said.

The guy from the road service, hung up on her! Bad move, her husband, is an attorney. The lawsuit papers were being drawn up on I-pages, on a mobile phone, posthaste. Retired attorneys have time on their hands; he can take that road service to the court and back again. Bad move. People!

If people would just use a paper map once and awhile, they would find addresses that lady on GPS gives up on. I could have told the road service guy that, but he was obviously thirty years old, and they know everything! If we told this story to our thirty-year-old children, they would say, in unison. "You all have cell phones, you could just call 911." "We are in the middle of the movie, sorry, gotta go"!

However, that day, all four cell phones probably added up to 50% power. Mine was at it's usual in the car travel reading of about 7% and due to die at any given time. Frack's was probably at 20%; she had been online shopping to settle her nerves. Bruce had sound notifications on that uses up power. He was ding, ding, dinging from under the car, in the snow. Mike was using his flashlight app; probably a million lumens drained that one.

There are new criteria on old people, if your cell phone is not fully charged, you are senile! If your cell phone has died from no power, an emergency service just lets you float to sea on the piece of ice your car is high centered on. And the polar bears have you for dinner.

Establish a New Doctor, Diagnosed S.A.D.

The annual physical exam takes on new meaning when you reach your 65th year. It becomes cursory; parts of you no longer need viewing or physical exam. For women, there are no more gynecological exams, just a quick peek to see if you have atrophied! "Atrophied, where did it go, I don't even use it anymore?" I was not prepared to have this exam, "What do you mean, you don't do a pelvic after age 65?" "Do you not care about that area? What if it falls out and rolls down the street, don't I have a problem?"

You are weighed and with your clothes on, for maximum digital read-out. Yet, you are asked to put on a gown and be naked at another point. I'd rather start naked and have a lower number to the weight, but what do I know? Then they measure your height. I've shrunk 3/4 of an inch, where did that go? They listen to your heart for a flashing moment,; if it's beating, you are great. If it isn't, that's the end of the exam.

Moving on to your breasts, those get full attention, and when you point out that the exam is painful, the doctor asks when the last time you were fitted for a bra?
Amazing, I camouflaged that forty-year-old Wacoal bar under my sweater and on top of my slacks when I undressed. How on earth did she see that poor dilapidated old thing? And, "No doctor, I have never been properly fitted in anything, much less my bra."

My legs were my pride and joy throughout my life up until menopause, and then all veins went south and bulged just right below my knee. Her exam hammer hit one of those veins, and now I have four hundred spider veins below the bulge.

On to the strength test; "Pull my hand," she said,. "Push my hand, pull my leg, push my leg, stand up, sit down." That was a football fight cheer wasn't it? I was drill team captain; I'm sure of it!

Somehow, I passed all of that and I told her, my right shoulder was hurting when it wasn't suppose to be hurting, I had just had rotator cuff repair surgery four months earlier. She said, ""I'm not an Orthopedic Surgeon, but that's not good". "So I'm sending you to one immediately." Why did I open my mouth?

She also shared with me that the Orthopedic Surgeon is "young." I immediately googled her bio. "Young, she's in high school at best, this is who is suppose to replace my shoulder with bolts and steel balls. I was thinking a few years experience.

The doctor then calmly said, "She's the only one who is accepting new, OLD patients." "Otherwise, you can be put on a piece of ice and floated out to sea for the polar bears! Take the young surgeon, your chances are better."

"Let's have a look at your eyes." " When was your last eye exam?" "Oh, let me think, I don't remember." "You have cataracts you know." I told her I thought there was a problem; everything looks like it has a thin film of Vaseline on it. I go through a box of eyeglass wipes daily. "That's cataracts," she said! "Go to this doctor, he's fourteen, but it's better than the polar bears".

This exam was almost over when the psychological questions had to be covered. Do you feel safe in your environment? Humm, now I had to ask that annoying question, Bruce asks of me. "What do you mean safe?"

"Are you happy moving all over the country like this?" "What do you mean happy?" And then the final diagnostic question: "Do you like grey skies, six feet of snow to each snowfall, the Polar Vortex temperatures of forty below zero and ten months of winter?" I was at a loss of words, so I cried.

The doctor declared at the end of the examination; I had Seasonal Affective Disorder. "You have SAD disorder, I'm ordering Vitamin D. She smiled and said, "Don't be SAD take Vitamin D, be GLAD!"

"Take all of your paperwork to the front desk and I will see you again in five years for your new physical exam protocol. NEXT"....... "Five years! The other end could be atrophied!

The Polar Vortex

The move to Minnesota was by far our stupidest one we've ever done. People our age don't migrate to Minnesota, they move to Florida. I didn't have much to say on this move, he jumped at the job and whatever it is he does at his work; he wanted to do in Minnesota.

I did nothing in Minnesota, except look out the dual pained, extra-insulated windows to the front and back yard of white marshmallow. If I did open the door; I was affronted with the Polar Vortex, I froze in place.

In twenty years, they had not seen a winter as the one we had the year we moved there. Forty below zero, locals called brisk! I did some research on the temperatures during the Polar Vortex.

If a person's face isn't covered with a mask of wool, your nose and ears can freeze to a crisp black in four to five minutes. If you breathe that temperature for longer than five minutes, your lungs shrink to the size of a jellybean and don't exchange warm air, thereby ending your life.

If you shovel snow after eating a meal, drinking an alcoholic beverage, hot or cold, not having enough sleep or too sleepy, you can trigger a heart attack. The snow needs to be evaluated before you shovel. Is it wet snow? Evidently wet is heavier, always was with a diaper. Does shoveling make your arm, jaw, chest or stomach hurt? You could be having a heart attack.

The trouble with that information is; we both hurt all the time. My arm, his shoulder, my stomach, his jaw, my ear, his eye, my nose, his back. How would we know?

The snow blower machine weighs two hundred pounds. Unless you take out a loan for the super duper, 115-24 model, electric starter, hand warmer, power steering, drift cutter model, you will kill yourself with the average department store model. It is wiser for our age group to call a snow removal service.

I looked out the window one day through the blizzard and here came the pick-up from the snow removal service. He was going 60 mph in a 15 mph neighborhood and slid right into our driveway. He jammed that truck into drive and I didn't hear the garage doors collapse, as he disappeared from view.

All of a sudden, here he came again, backwards out to the street and another run up the driveway. He pushed mountains of snow over into the neighbors yard, covered the fire hydrant, came back and pushed another mountain of snow to the center of our yard, taking out the bushes underneath. Of course, Bruce's Christmas lights had to have been toast after that maneuver.

I watched him run up and down several times, then with the speed of lightening, he jumped out of the truck, grabbed his mega shovel and cleared the walkway in one fell swoop. He ran back to the truck, grabbed a box of ice melt and started flinging it from side to side. He jumped into the pick-up, hung his arm out the window with his digital camera, took a picture of his fine job and burned rubber on the snow down the street.

It was my entertainment for the week, it's a mini series now, and I watch him weekly.

He doesn't even collect money at the door. About an hour after he leaves, a bell goes off on my computer, there's an email from his company. Click here if you approve his job and he is paid right onto my credit card. Click here if you disapprove and you get new medical insurance. Amazing....

What makes me think I'm Forty?

When I was forty, I could unpack from a cross-country move in three days, fix dinner for ten people in thirty minutes, and give birth while brushing my teeth. Now, this last move has taken me down.

It has been three months and cob webs are forming on the stacked unpacked boxes in the garage, the basement is impassable with more unpacked boxes and two closets have the clothes laying on the floor, I haven't found the box of hangers, yet, I'm using tree branches.

Had I clicked on the "pack and unpack for you" button on the moving company website, it would have been a different situation. I was doomed; there was no end to this move, I had no life, I was a victim of my own doing.

After consulting with a Taro reader, having my

palms read, a few self help books, and talking to the walls; I decided the majority of my prized household belongings needed to go. How they should go was my dilemma.

I could box them up again and ship to each of my children, the postage alone, would be their inheritance. Or, I could put it all on the Internet selling sites and have complete strangers wandering throughout the house, casing it for a future break-in. I might try a consignment store, but here again, I would have to re-box it, dry clean it, press it again and polish it before they will even look at it, and all items have to be on wooden hangers, facing east!

There are the thrift store trucks that say, just call us; we pick up your treasures. That's not as simple as they advertise. They email you their criteria list, read before we come for your treasures.

It is a laundry list of do's and don't s.
1. Pack in our provided lunch size bags, fold and staple the top of each bag.

2. Do not donate any perishable items, go ahead and eat them before we arrive.

3. Separate diamonds from junk jewelry, untangle all gold necklaces, we don't want to do it, either!

4. If any of your kitchen appliances are older than three years, we don't want them, antique kitchen pots and pans won't sell.

5. No Brass items that went out years ago.

6. No collections of coffee cups, they only did that in the sixties.

7. Anything avocado green, harvest gold or turquoise will not sell.

The young busy housewife of today will not polish sterling silver; forget that, she's a paper plate kind of woman. Your Waterford collection, they don't like that either. Your grandmother's tatted tablecloths are passé, only placemats accepted. No cloth napkins, it's a disposable world; have to think of the landfills!

Anything you have handmade, such as paintings, ceramic ashtrays, play dough art, pop cycle stick birdhouses or knitted items are not accepted.

We will, however, accept savings bonds, passwords to your bank accounts, gold and silver coin collections, cash in the stapled lunch bags.

This left me with only one choice to the unpacked items in this 4000 square foot house. I will return to RV life, 400 square feet, it is manageable for this time in my life.

I have a plan, drag out the survival bag in the back of the car, with kindling, waterproof matches, a canister of kerosene to go and set the house on fire! It is the only solution. This is basic chemistry...The Solution to Pollution is Dilution!

Fire dilutes to ashes...that makes me think, I don't have the advanced directive finalized either.

We're Engaged

With six girls, Bruce and I are in forever plan a wedding mode. I have reams of notebooks with invoices for everything from chocolate dipped roses to homemade jam recipes for favors. I have color schemes from black and white, (the bride wears white; you want me as the Mother of the groom to wear black?) to lemon yellow, "Mom you can wear my other color orange," to sky blue and grey (you guessed it; I was to wear grey).

When we get the excited call for permission to marry another one of our girls, I just want to know the color scheme. I don't care how in love they are; I can't find a dress in my size, in lime green.

I have made wedding cakes for almost all of them now. I have had every cake disaster known to the bakery world. The first cake creation had a water fountain at the base of the three tiers. I froze the cake because it had whipped cream frosting on it, and that would assure it being fresh and no worries.

Trouble was, it sat in the corner window on display before the wedding, fountain flowing and it thawed. The top layer took a mid-air flip and landed top down onto the carpet. My husband came to me stark naked screaming, "OMG, the cake fell over!" "Why were you looking at the cake naked?" was I all I could say.

At the last wedding, I laid out my husband's suit, tie, shoes and socks. All he had to do was put them get dressed. His suit was beige; he had new brown shoes. He came out to have his boutonniere pinned on, and I looked down at his feet with black shoes on, outlined with mud from the night before climb to the rehearsal in the woods. "Ok, surprise me, why do you have on black shoes?"

"Now honey," he said, "There was a small problem." "The shoe box had two right shoes in it." " I don't care, go back and put them on, you can't wear muddy black shoes!" His feet do have some deformity from that command.

Meeting the in-laws is a nerve-wracking experience. "I'm the old Mother, she's so perky." "Look at her hair, it's a black shiny, no hair out of place wonder." Mine is dishwater blonde, subject to the slightest puff of air, and I look like the aftermath of a tornado.

Or, "She is so tiny, what size is she, a two?" I didn't wear that size when I was born. "What did you say, she's ten years older than me, and she hikes Mt Everest and rides on camels." Oh dear, what will I talk about?

I can't get up half a flight of stairs without an asthma attack, and the only thing I will ride is around the block in my Escalade. Bruce has no problem, he bonds with anyone., he talks to anyone who will listen and eats whatever they put in front of him. He can't be rejected.

We had one wedding at our house, one year and the bachelor party was the night before the wedding. No one would ever fess up as to who planned that fiasco. All the guys jumped into my van including the father of the bride, (my guy) and took off to drink themselves into unconscious states. The story changes every year, but the reality was they were all sick to a toxic point, driving drunk and should have been arrested.

My son missed the wedding of one of his sisters. He barfed for two consecutive days and put on half a tuxedo the day of the wedding, crawled to the front door and was carried back to bed.

My husband made everyone sign in blood from the bachelor party to not tell mom the van was a cesspool of vomit. There was beer bottles hidden inside the hubcaps and a case of evergreen scented little trees stashed under the drivers seat. Did they think I wouldn't notice?

The groom, I took aside and instructed him to shove a suppository up his backside for nausea just to get to the altar. The bride was a puddle of tears, the mother of the groom was glaring, the father of the groom was laughing; he chose not to go to the bachelor party.

The dinner no one remembers. I made that wedding cake and covered the icing with white chocolate curls. I remember just sitting beside it and picking off chocolate curls to dunk into my champagne glass, while I wondered why men and women get married in the first place.

Our eldest girl and our son both decided to get married sixteen days apart! The rationale to that was the grandparents were coming from out of state and the second wedding they wouldn't be able to come back for, so let's just have two weddings!

Oh no, they couldn't have a double wedding. My daughter wanted pink blush and blush and flowing chiffon everywhere, and prime rib with au jus juice.

My son wanted a black and white ceremony in the evening, in our back yard with all of Dad's white Christmas twinkle lights, strung everywhere.

Bruce needed to be medicated to untangle those lights in the July heat.

"Mom, this would be so cool, paint the porch black and sprinkle it with glitter, hang a disco ball and turn up the music until the police come." "Don't worry about food, just order keg-gars!" "What's a keg-gar, son?"

How is it possible, with all the bridal shops and department stores available to find wedding attire; I could get dressed in a black chiffon skirt and white brocade jacket, black satin heels, step into the church and the mother of the groom had on the same outfit, same shoes? Of course, she out shined me; she had that black shiny, no out of place bouffant hair do, and I had on a hat that sat on my head as cockeyed as the whole situation.

I'm a Baby Boomer Grandma

Baby boomers are the welcome home babies of World War II. Now we are the largest segment of society, being cared for by children doctors, being written about by children journalists and being readied for the retirement home by our children.

This is a massive dose of reality or dementia, however; one wants to define it. Baby boomers have infinite amounts of wisdom; millenniums don't want to hear it.

In our day, when we realized we were expecting a baby, three rabbits had died in the laboratory, two months of vomiting had occurred, and we bought the newly padded bras to form a barrier from the sorest breasts we had ever known.

We called our mothers to hear their horrifying tales of childbirth. Mine said to me, "Oh I knew it was a boy, I carried him very high, all the girls were low and low back pain." Humm, I carried all my girls high and had the worst back pain with the boy! No empirical science there.

In my day, (boy there is the dated phrase, get ready for this), we did not get to know the babies sex until we heard the cry in the delivery room.

Our prep time as they call it now, consisted of having a baby shower; see what you need after that. The nursery was either yellow or mint green, how stupid to paint it pink, if a boy pops out. Our Mothers and Grandmothers gave us little white outfits and bonnets and lace shawl blankets.

We had to stock up on cloth diapers and large safety pins, diaper pail, and a huge plastic diaper clip to rinse the poop diapers out in the toilet before they went into the pail! Don't even ask about the pail to the washing machine process, it was gross. I usually ran two empty loads following the diaper load, to clean the machine for family laundry use. They hadn't invented the plug in all day deodorizer, in fresh linen or sunshine floral. I had to pour liquid bleach on the floor and kill the smell with another smell.

We carried the baby in our arms, and in our laps for the ride home. The proud new father had his box of cigars at the ready for light up in the hospital. He passed them out to the staff, and everyone lit up. We were wheeled out of the hospital in a cloud of smoke to raise our new little charge.

Those babies all lived. They became asthmatics true, from the cigar smoke. They had a bump or two from no car seats. One of my toddlers had a fetish to the car door handle, she finally opened the door in the backseat and as I glanced into the side rear view mirror, there she was, rolling down the boulevard. True, if safety latches had been there that would not have happened. They probably would have shown more parental love, if we had dressed them in red, instead of mint green.

A few of them got their heads stuck in the crib slats, which could have been a better design. I had one child fairly traumatized from potty training on the new snap on potty seat to the toilet. It unsnapped and we fished her out of the toilet. One of my babies wasn't ready for strained carrot baby food. She turned orange and had a full body rash, the doctor said, "Ease up on the carrots!"

Dad laid one of the babies on the waterbed and then did his usual belly flop into bed. The baby sailed across the room and landed in a pile of dirty clothes. (Who says, the laundry has to be done all the time, it saved her life?)

Now a day, (still dating myself) the new mother knows when she is pregnant by her cell phone app. It tells her when she is fertile, when she needs to grab her husband and baby make, and it announces the event to everyone except those blocked from the account. She can go into her medical account online and order nausea pills delivered to her doorstep.

The new parents of today are told the sex of the child at twenty weeks. They can take their sonogram pictures to go and post on social media.

They can Skype the baby and avoid thumb sucking before the baby even enters the world, saying, "No, no, no don't suck your thumb!" They can play the music they want the baby to listen to as a teenager (good luck on that!) They can create a virtual dance theatre for their little one, inside the womb. Never mind, if the baby is rocking out,; the mother's ribs will be broken at some point, the technology is fabulous.

The babies of today are not held as yesteryear, they are in body slings called Bjorns! They don't recline; the baby faces outward or faces toward the mother and suffocates! Either way, the new mother cannot seem to remember to put a hat on those infants. Mother is always in trendy coat, infinity tied scarf, hat and gloves herself, but baby is slung out to the world in short sleeve onesies!

The diapers of today are state of the art, they have a yellow line down the center of the paper diaper; it turns blue when wet. No need to stick your finger in the side and come out with any surprise.

Here's a footnote for the young bunch of environmentalists who want me to separate my cans, glasses, plastic bottles, and newspapers. And then scrub them out, dry them, separate again and take them to the transfer trash station.

I ask you my darlings; these diapers are PLASTIC and PAPER, and they are full of POOP. They do not disintegrate they pile up in landfills. Your baby will use about eight thousand disposable diapers before training pants. Sixteen thousand, if you don't get around to potty training until age four. You need to feel as guilty as you make me feel about those darn bottles, cans and papers.

BTW, (I have to express in generational X and Y talk), did you know, paper diapers are killing the wildlife in Ittoqqortoormiit, Greenland? The seas surrounding it are almost perpetually frozen, but your discarded plastic, paper diapers are sliding off the ice, and the polar bears are eating them, it's a disaster!

I had seven children and only one stroller; that was for number five or six. It was a fold up umbrella stroller that did carry the infant. If they fell asleep, I was reduced to pushing it onto the back wheels. I would lean down and push until the spasms in my back became unbearable. I watched a woman, tie her umbrella stroller to her car, to keep the baby sleeping. Only a female judge would understand that one!

The parent of today has a motorized, three wheel stroller that converts to a bed, car seat and a kitchenette all in one. There is a shelf for the cell phone holder and charger, two cup coffee holder and bottle warmer, mini refrigerator, diaper bag holder, and bag dispenser for used diapers. Throw them in the doggie pooh containers, as you stroll by, I guess.

These three wheel wonders have a sunshade, a rain shade, and a snow cover, the interior is temperature controlled. There is an option if you want to download an app, you can see the baby inside!

No need for Mother to come soothe the nerves of the new mother of today. She has had pre-natal training, post natal, pre lactation classes, post pump classes, pre day care evaluation, Lamaze classes, mothering the mother and bonding classes, pregnancy yoga and a labor Doula! Who needs Mother? Skype me occasionally.

Understanding the X's and Y's

In addition to being called a senior, moderately obese, a degenerative mess, in need of hearing aids, and over the hill. Add to that description, I am a middle age person born one year ahead of the Baby Boomers, making me a Mature/Silents generation.

The generational characteristic study is what all companies use now to hire and understand their employees. Gone are the days; you had an interview, put the person to work and decided if they were doing the job. Now the employer must understand and meet the emotional needs of their new hire.

I am pre-feminism according to my generational profile, no wonder I never understood Helen Gurleys, bra burning days. The tie dying hippie group, I could not relate to either. I cannot sit still to Big Band Swing music. I could jitterbug up and down the street., all night long in my youth. My generation of Mature/Silents read the newspaper front to back. I think I broke the mold; I don't read the newspaper or line the birdcage with it afterwards, I read it online, so there!

My kids are Xs and Ys and after a short google search, I can tell you they all fit their defined generational characteristics. Generation X's (born between 1965 - 1977) don't want or need face time.

This explains how we could all live in the same town; they would just drive right by our house and not even swing in for a cup of coffee. I thought it was because I brewed Folgers's in a real coffee pot, and they use pods. But no, it's because they don't want or need face time. Gen X-er's as they call themselves are supreme skeptics and cynics. Now that explains they're not eating Brussels sprouts when they were young. They thought I was trying to kill them!

But Generation Y or the Millennial's good grief! They have to be praised daily and coached. And we were considered to be helicopter parents! I've never even been in a helicopter. I resent this; it's defining me as overprotective and excessively indulgent to the Y's.

After the toddler X-er, fell out of the car and rolled down the street, it is true, I became a paranoid protector. I strapped her to my back and wouldn't let her have a butter knife until her wedding dinner. Ok, I'm defined by my generation; it says I'm cautious.

I don't know who thinks up this stuff, but if these X's and Y's think the helicopter is going to come rescue them, they need to read about the mature/silent group. The characteristic states, "We are the richest, freest spending retirees in history". Therefore, our money goes to ourselves, not the alphabet.

I hope the X's, Y's, and Z's can understand that and not need therapy. Now if they want to come over and share alphabet soup with me, we are all on board.

Our grandchildren are the Z's, finally a description that fits. They are described as having their faces into a technology gadget. They eat with the cell phone one inch from their eyes, using the base of the phone as a napkin. They hang in a bean chair completely zzz-mesmerized in X-box. Their characteristic profile states, they will be worldlier than any other generation.

Well, I guess; their videos are more violent than any war my dad or husband served in to date. There are supposed to be parental controls to monitor this video phenomenon.

It appears the parent has to be an alpha dog and take charge. If I was a helicopter parent, then the Y's are submarines! They are so under water; they have all drowned.

These Z's have bedrooms outfitted like command posts for Norad. The alpha dog has to go to boot camp and learn how to pass lock the router and confiscate the console!

No wonder none of the grand kids wants to come visit Grandma and Grandpa. All that we have to offer is one 42" TV screen. And, Grandpa has the remote control surgically stitched to his hand, no choice there. Grandma makes hot chocolate and homemade marshmallows for her darling grandchildren, neither of which any of those kids has ever had.

"OMG, Grandma, no bull drink and sushi?" How do we explain to them? "Your Grandma got high on second hand pot smoke in Amsterdam, and she hates raw fish, you could offer her Beluga caviar and she would toss it in the recycle bin."

"Grandpa is diabetic, he can't have white rice and who in their right mind wants to chew on seaweed?"

Here's an idea to the Z's, it's great kids. You take one of Grandma's homemade marshmallows; put it on a stick over a campfire, (or the Bunsen burner in your room). Roast it until all gooey. Then take a graham cracker and place a marshmallow on top of a cracker, add a square of chocolate, top it with another cracker. "Eat it!!!" "I know, it's to die for." "Grandma and Grandpa, hands down favor it over seaweed!"

Hidden Jewels in the Consignment Store

There is a point in your life when you can eyeball quality. I can go to a garage sale and see the Waterford vase on the back table next to the tub of outgrown snickers. The trick to the garage sale bartering game is not to let the young housewife trying to sell her Mothers cast-offs, know what I am thinking. She is having a garage sale to have money to go to a music concert.

I am on a quest for the three hundred dollar Waterford vase marked three dollars. I pick through the old smelly snickers, asking if they are all twenty-five cents a pair. And then casually say, "Would you take two dollars for the glass vase?" She smiles and says, "Sure, that old thing, I hated it." "We got that for a wedding present."

Without drawing a new breath, she says to me, "You want to see my wedding dress?" "I dyed it yellow and made it into a short dress for a girlfriend's Japanese divorce party, they wear yellow and bring a mallet to crush their rings, isn't that cool?" " I just want fifteen dollars for it." "My goodness dear, that is lovely lace what did that dress cost, when it was a wedding dress?" "Oh, I think Mom said about seventy-eight hundred dollars." "I'll take it too, dear." (I'll bleach it!!)

I have two close friends who are thrift store queens; I call them. In defense of me, I have cataracts; I have a thin film of Vaseline I look through every day, that hinders me when thrift shopping. I can carefully rummage through a rack of clothes and declare it all just old clothes and then my friend NancyJean steps up to the rack and finds the Bob Mackie original.

She found a cowhide pocket book one time, took it to her shoe shop repair man to have a strap put on it, he looked at her and asked her if she knew what she had? She would say, yes she did know, but there is no cowgirl in her, so I know she did not. The shoe shop man said to her, "It's worth about twelve hundred dollars lady!"

She is the thrift shopper who can find a jacket for a dollar and a quarter on the 75% off day and there is ten thousand dollar ring in the side pocket.

Same thing with my friend across the country in Maine; she marks her territory in her church thrift shop, and when they see her coming, those little old volunteer ladies buckle. She can spot the twenty-five cent teacup that is English Bone china from the Queens collection, from across the room. As she holds up a North Face down coat, never worn for five dollars. I cannot even compete with that!!

If we ever drive to Maine instead of fly, I do have a complete set of German Havilland Bone China dishes, service for twelve, maybe eleven in her basement, which I picked up from that thrift shop. That is a good friend who will hold your stash for you. She did text me recently that the space is available six more months, then the dishes go back to the thrift shop, or she will set her table for

Easter dinner with them and stuff them into her daughters Easter basket.

I came across a new concept recently. A young woman started a baby resale store. She obviously knew none of the mothers of today would buy anything used, so she only accepts baby items that have been worn to take a professional picture in or still have the tags on them. Clothes that the baby outgrew before they put it on them. Cleaver, right?

The store is bulging with clothes, cribs, strollers, car seats, toys and extra children. Children are not selling well, but the clothes; Grandmas are stuffing their shopping bags full.

I have been told you take the clothes home; hand washes them, steam them and fold them into a Nordie box. Attach a radio-frequency identification tag, from Nordie or Saks, to each item. Good to go.....baby outgrows them in thirty minutes, Grandma saves her money to go on another cruise. It works for me.

People do act differently in a consignment store than Sak's, for instance. In Sak's, they walk about the store with a purpose. Although, I'm not sure if they are customers or models for the store, they both look like manikins.

Elegant looking women come in fresh from the spa; hair newly colored, nails shining brightly; their drivers have had the three carat diamond ring polished during the mani; they are ready to drop the big bucks. Their clothes are completely coordinated in color and latest style.

I could put on their same outfit, and somehow I would look like I was trying to fool myself in the junior petite department. Clerks always just give you a look when your body doesn't match the size you are thumbing through on the rack.

I respond with my usual comeback, "I've been on steroids for months, but I'm trying to lose weight. Or, "I'm just looking for one of my daughters". Both comments always get the same response from the clerk.

"Oh yes, those medicine are terrible aren't they? Or, How sweet of you shopping for your daughter, is it her sweet sixteen birthday?" "No, she's forty, she's in denial."

In high school, all the girls had this smooth flip back to their hair; I don't know how they did it. It flipped back or flipped up; the best mine would do was frizz or look like it just came out of the rollers and froze in a tootsie roll configuration.

There was that collegiate look, a soft cashmere sweater and plaid skirt with penny loafers. And the necklace with a circle on it! Everyone had that necklace, except me. I shopped until I dropped one time looking for that circle necklace. The closest I could find was a poodle hanging off the chain.

"Sorry," the clerk would say, "We sold the last cheerleader smooth style sweater, would you like this grey fisherman's cable knit sweater?" "We have rubber fishing waders on sale too!"

In the consignment store, however, it is a mix and match wonderland of hoodies and jeans customers. Turn around, and someone has on your donated funeral suit. Not the wedding dress, our generation hermetically sealed them in boxes, just in case our daughters wanted to wear them, someday.

They don't, they don't even want the something new, old or blue. There is a whole section in the consignment store of new; never worn bridal garters, earrings, mother's string of pearls, handkerchiefs, and veils.

Veils are out, birdcages are in! It's shocking to a mother who watched Sound of Music a hundred times; Maria's veil was our dream wedding. How can they not want a veil?

Of course, my dad stepped on mine going down the aisle; the whole thing was sliding toward the bouquet in my hands. He was supposed to pull it back and give me a kiss goodbye; we rehearsed the whole thing the day before. I had so much tulle in my face I couldn't find my groom; maybe the birdcage is better.

On one shopping day, I was happily doing my ram sacking of household items when I turned around, and a woman was upside down in a recliner. Her legs were straight up in the air, and she was moaning. I couldn't help her; I had a bad shoulder, what could I do? Everyone else must have had bad shoulders; we all just looked at her! The store clerk didn't ask if she was hurt, she just said, "Didn't you see the DO NOT SIT sign on the chair?"

About that time, my husband entered the store wanting to know what was taking me so long. "What do you mean, what am I doing, there's a lady stuck in that chair!" He righted her up as if she was a bulldozer that had turned over on the road.

She didn't thank him, she just said, "I'm not

buying that thing, it's unreliable!" He calmly said to her, "Probably why it's priced at a dollar."

On the way out of the store after that incident, I passed a hand carved little horse with a real horsehair tail. I stopped to look at it, and Bruce threatened to put me in that recliner if I didn't head for the car and bypass that little jewel of a find.

I will shop there when he's having his annual colonoscopy!

Miss Mary, You Should Have Stayed in the South

We spent a few months in the South; the people are just amazing. Men of all ages open doors for women of all ages. I'm used to being crushed in the mob at Wal-Mart. However, my first day in the South, a man was halfway to his car, he saw me headed for the door to the hardware store, turned around and walked back to open the door for me! I asked him if he'd marry me!

I thought of my one son out in Orange County, California.... I used to take him by the ear and say to him at six years of age, you better be doing this son, you have to open the door for ladies, that is what gentlemen does. He would look up at me and say, "I didn't do anything Mommy, she did it!"

Wonder what the Southern Moms did to get that point across; maybe they threatened their sons with a haircut? "Yes, ma'am, just don't put the bowl on my head and give me a haircut, I'll open doors for life!"

I drove home that day and expected Bruce to open the bathroom door for me, the car door, and the door to the campground laundry. I used the silent treatment method; I just stood there waiting for him to open whatever. And he just stood there and looked at me, saying, "What did you forget?"

The little town we were in for Bruce's job had one drive-through dry cleaner. I would pull in to drop off a load of clothes and this lady with no teeth would come out smiling ear to ear, saying, "Hey Miss Mary." "How are ya'll today, did you get over your cold, how are the kids, are ya'll doing, ok out there at the campground, do you need anything?"

"We have a special this week, if someone dies and ya'll need to go for the funeral, we dry clean for free!" I had to admit; no one had ever said that to me, and it was good to know that was available for me.

Lunch in the South is not a ham and cheese on rye sandwich. Everywhere you could eat; it was the same thing. A hot buffet of fried chicken, collard greens, mashed potatoes, sweet potatoes, mac'n'cheese, okra, and banana pudding.

The only drink available was sweet tea. That is not my mother's version of three teaspoons of sugar in a glass of iced tea. That is simple syrup by the quart mixed into the tea, add ice and go into a diabetic coma.

Burnt sugar cake, is the oldest recipe I know. I hadn't had it since I was a child, and my mother made it. In the South, it is boxed and ready to go to the roadside peach stand. Bruce hadn't even heard of it; he is such a hang ten, California boy. He is diabetic too, so I ate his portion; he will never know how good it is.

Bruce had a fellow co-worker at work that did not want to camp in the woods like we were doing, so he bought a South Carolina home. Three thousand square feet of a house for one person! He called it the ranch. He was from California too; they buy a house at the square foot price. "Wow, that's only $88 a square foot, get it quick, it's only been on the market four years, what's wrong with these people," he would say?

We all decided to work together and re-model his new old home and flip it, making a fortune. The house had been on the market for over two years. The flip it concept applies to ocean front property, he was a Californian, it's all about dollars per square foot. Not about anything making sense.

He hired a contractor and away he went, in one week he had spent 100K. I used to say to him, what's new at the ranch? And he would say, "I changed out all the windows and pipes under the house and new gutters."

Humm, any woman, will grab up that remodel. "Maybe you should change that 1920 velvet wallpaper in the living room?" He came up with the bright idea for me to have something to do while the guys were at work. "Why don't you wallpaper for me, Miss Mary?"

I don't know my limitations; I just thrive on adventure!! I papered his laundry room, outstanding look! I started the kitchen nook and then a sharp pain stabbed at my shoulder, followed by paralysis and an inability to even lift my dinner fork. I had a problem.

I went to an Orthopedic Surgeon, who, by the way, was drop dead good looking, and he said, my shoulder was done for, "It's Rotator Cuff tear!" I thought that was what football players got! "What do we do?"

"Surgery, you will be in a brace eight weeks, rehab the rest of your life and don't lift anything heavier than your dinner fork!

That put a crimp in my style; I don't care about flipping anything, I never did learn to flip the bird. I don't even know how to rock, paper, scissors. I left the South for the Southerners to remodel, buy new, save the Rotator cuff.

My friend Patty came to see me while we were in South Carolina. She wanted to spend the night in our RV. She and her husband were helping her son make a cross country move; she existed left or north or some direction in Charleston from her family, to come see us. She told them she'd catch up with them after our visit!

She thinks everything is as well secured as Disneyland, if it is a tourist attraction. She had to see the plantation swamp preserve in downtown Hartsville, in the less than eight hours we had together. Then she would rendezvous with her family again and continue her road trip.

I told her the swamp tour was self-guided, gave her my cactus walking stick and we were off to see the swamp. She took off again, bouncing along on the wood sidewalk built over the swamp; I was bringing up the rear with another stick ready to fight off water moccasins and alligators.

There were signs everywhere, "Don't harm the natural animals of the swamp, you as man we could care less about!" See if I donate to the cash box at the top of the stairs on the way out, save the water moccasin over me?"

Our cell phones wouldn't work as we headed deeper into the swamp, the sky went away; we could only see vines and critters run back and forth on them as we kept going. This time Patty changed gears, she turned and said, "I don't think I should have worn flip flops, do you think we should go back?

Well, I said, "We took that fork in the road about two hours back, and I can't find us on the self guided walking map. I don't think you should worry about flip-flops. I think we are hopelessly lost in a swamp!"

"I could have taken you to lunch, for all you can eat collard buffet." "We would have had a chance of survival, now I have to rely on my reality show survival techniques."

"Grab a leaf off the tree, and I'll lay a flat sewing needle from my purse on it and that will tell us our direction." "The alligator just ate it, now we really are lost," I said.

At the top of the staircase after we followed a tame deer from the swamp, she had 35 cell phone voice messages from her husband, "Where are you, we are waiting for you?"

I don't think she shared that visit with him, I know I left out a lot of information to Bruce that night. "What did you and Patty do today," he asked. "We caught a movie in town, nothing exciting, dear!"

Surgery Again?

I was a nurse in another life. I keep my license active; I don't know why. I have either forgotten all that I knew or the new groups of medical professionals are a breed of their own, and they have changed all the medical information, I once knew.

The first time around of my nursing life, I put my starched white cap on my head, put on my white uniform and shimmied into my white hose with seams up the back of my leg. We were identified by the color of the band of velvet on our caps. Black band, a registered nurse, grey, a licensed practical nurse, no band or cap, not a nurse. The aides were in white uniforms, no caps. The candy strippers were about twelve years old and were identified by a magazine cart. Doctors were in their white coats with monogrammed signature names on their top pocket of their lab coats. All was well, we all knew who did what!

Now it is chaos! Every healthcare professional is

in black, red, purple or blue scrubs. How is an old person suppose to know she just told the physical therapist in blue; she was constipated? She asked for pain medicine from the guy in black and he was the hospital maintenance man. She wanted coffee black instead of prune juice and the doctor glared at her, he was in his golf attire; dietary wears the same outfit. The senior keeps looking for a nurse with her white uniform and cap and she is long gone.

Having a work-up done for an impending surgery can put a senior into Xanax territory. Slowly you come to grips with the fact your doctor resembles your high school grandchild in appearance. For myself, I go deep into Internet investigation of all of their credentials and grades. If they pass my intrusion into their school records, are duly licensed and have fellowship in their field of medicine. I feel fairly certain they are in the know, and I will proceed further for an examination.

And then I wait in their exam room to meet them.

If I have to sit there in a flimsy gown with no back and I am unable to even tie it closed for more than thirty minutes, the notches just start going down on my evaluation of this doctor.

If the nurse closes the door and I am in there alone with a sign taped on the back of the exam room," PLEASE TELL THE NURSE IF YOU HAVE A DIRTY DIAPER SO IT CAN BE DISPOSED OF PROPERLY." (With a picture of a little black skunk on the sign). The notch is lowered further.

If this drags onto an hour of waiting, my claustrophobic personality comes out, and I do not care if the sign over the counter says for staff only. I will start stuffing my clothes pockets with Q-tips, tongue depressors, band aides, rolls of gauze and syringes, until I empty the place.

I will put my clothes back on and calmly walk right past that new doctor with his or her hand extended for a handshake, as we pass each other through the door.

If all goes well and I can be seen in a timely manner, then I try to follow this doctor's instructions.

Each exam room has a computer in it now; on the screen is my life with MRI pictures included. I had to be medicated and blindfolded to go through an MRI. Without Elvis singing to me, I never would have made it. And now the doctor wanted to go over the findings of that experience. It just took me back to the moment of the clanging in that tube...But ok, go ahead, what's wrong?

They need to do the surgery again!! "Are you kidding me?" My shoulder came completely apart and this time, they will go in and titanium me to the point I will have to be escorted through airport security for life!

At the conclusion of the pre-op exam, the doctor handed me my instructions, complete with the color-coding of the various departments to go to for my tests. Follow the yellow line to the lab, the black line to X-ray, green line to pulmonary studies, blue to EKG, red for Pharmacy, and finally, the white line to the Chaplain.

I got through the blood draw; those tests take awhile to come back. I had a chest X-ray, no problem. I flunked the pulmonary study. The EKG was borderline or else they ran out of ink for the graph paper. But the topper was the Chaplain; he would not see me without the Advanced Directive!

They keep telling me I have rights!! I'll go to the hospital Administrator and get this straightened out or else I will call my Maine lawyer!

The days are gone to check in the day before and get comfortable for your surgery tomorrow morning at the hospital. Oh no, your surgery is at 7:30 AM be at the hospital at 5:30 AM. You cannot have anything to eat or drink after midnight, but it is ok to drink water or have black coffee. What Starbuck's is open at 5:00 AM for a drive through cup on the way to the operating room?

I have a set of papers ready for signature from a responsible medical staff member. Since I've been asked to sign the same form, check the same boxes on that format every place they have sent me. I believe they can sign one form for me.

I want my coffee with French Vanilla cream in it as soon as they see my eyelids open. If non-responsive, have Bruce hold a straw and feed it to me, I want my coffee. I want a signature, date and time, also print on the line if you are MD, RN or the outside window washer. I want to know who was responsible for my cup of coffee.

Do not allow the Anesthesiologist to sign that form, he administers Versed, he knows I won't remember my coffee.

Sleeping Upright

No pre op instructions stated that following the surgical procedure, the moon aligns with the stars and the Universe puts out a gravitational command that your body will not be able to lay down in a prone position. You will not sleep on a bed, couch or hammock, you can only sleep sitting up.

I'm a resourceful person, maybe if I use the baby boppy pillow. I could sink the shoulder into that pillow like it was nursing and fool it to where I could lay down and sleep. Not a good idea, once you try to get down the coming back up requires the rest of the bottle of Dilaudid.

I had to research how I can sleep for six weeks and not be in my bed. No one lays on the toilet. I could not bend with the contraption brace that wanted on me 24 seven that meant I couldn't hang on the kitchen counter with a pillow. I had to figure this out; my neighbor said "My husband sleeps all day and half the night in his recliner".

There it is, a recliner, I thought they went out with the harvest gold carpet. They seem to be alive and thriving in the furniture stores and on the RV assembly line.

My first go around with shoulder surgery; we were living in the RV. Four hundred square feet of undeniable homey comfort, unless you are living in pain, then the RV is a hellhole.

There were two recliners in the living room area (all recreational vehicle furniture is designed for children). They look like recliners, however, upon measurement, they hold half a person. They are bolted to the floor, and they have manual wood handles on the right side of the recliner, that requires a stiff jerking motion to operate.

My suggestion, have left shoulder surgery, it may not address the right shoulder pain, but at least you can operate the recliner.

When you live in an RV, you never test out the recliners. It is a full time job to get the rig set-up and keep operating. You are outside hours on end, hooking up, as they say, in full timer language.

First comes the flipping of the coin to see who gets the fun job of attaching the sewer hose. Then it is plug the mega power hose into a 500-volt station that appears to be wet from the rain a few minutes ago. "You do it, you're the Electrical Engineer."

When parking the rig, as you are screaming at each other to move a little to the left or right, walkie-talkies save marriages in RV living. "What did you say?" I said "'Left, not right, you just ran into that four million dollar rig!." Definitely use walkie-talkies.

The awning has to be lowered, following the checklist order, as that hidden balloon is full of water and whoever is lowering it will be drenched. I laminated that checklist; he never remembers to use it.

Someone has to roll out the forty feet of artificial turf, gives it a manicured look opposed to gravel or dirt. That rug has to be secured with a sledgehammer and railroad stakes for occasional wind gusts. If you have run into the neighbors rig, they do not like you and if your turf flies over into their turf, it's a war!

You think you are finished and then you go inside. It is pitch dark because the slides are still in and it's about eighteen inches wide to maneuver yourself to the control panel and start moving the sliders out!

Caution, your other half needs to be inside also. I took two inches off of Bruce's height one time, moving the kitchen slide out over his head. Flip on the clean water, start the icemaker; you get about six cubes per day that needs to get started. Unpack everything you secured for bumping down the road; realize half of that you will be tossing. It was broken to smithereens!

Insert a TV dinner into the microwave and it is rock, paper, scissors for who gets the restricted flow of hot water coming from the two-gallon tank for a shower. Then off to bed, there is no time to sit in the undersized recliners.

I thought we had it covered for my place to sleep after the surgery, because we had the recliners. Once I came back from a outpatient procedure, Bruce guided me to the chair for my continual stay for six weeks.

I had a cowbell to call him to yank the side handle and jettison me up for bathing and bathroom needs. I was helpless. Once I was down, I was there until he set it in another position. If I wanted to be up, he was outside wandering and talking, if I wanted to sleep he had the TV blaring. I stayed heavily drugged for the time I needed to be in the recliner.

This surgery, our lesson learned, all stoppers have been pulled, the recliner we got was top of the line leather. It was electrically controlled, had a massage mode remote control. A side console with hidden storage unit for stashed Necco's and Rollo's.

There were two-cup holders and remote control center for the TV, coffee pot and the microwave. My medications were dispensed in a battery operated plastic carousel. No overdosing with that little invention.

Bruce rigged up a clear hose from the water dispenser on the refrigerator, direct to the chair; turn a diverter valve and I had ice water at the ready, or prune juice.

That man realized he was at my beck and call the first time around. This ingenious new set-up allowed him to be in his chair with his remote for his football game and occasionally glimpse over at my contraption to see if anything was leaking or malfunctioning.

He has tried to patent his invention; he just does not have the kinks worked out of it yet. That water dispensing idea of his with the hose, he mistakenly connected it to a small keg of beer in the refrigerator and I did overdose!

Paint a Picture or The House

I have noticed through the years that when the celebrities or politicians retire, they start painting pictures. Red Skelton probably made more money with his oil paintings of clowns; than his stand up comedy ever brought him. Who knew, it's a retirement gene? My mother painted oils freehanded; I must have the gene!

She was pretty good with landscapes and animals. Invariably, when she drew a person, her proportions were way off. Especially the hands, she did a nude woman of probably of her best friend; the woman's hands looked like that of an old man they unwrapped from the mummy tomb. She nailed the bosom, and that was all that my dad cared about.

That oil painting done on black velvet was an eight-foot long by four foot high bar nude for his new full size basement bar he constructed himself. Between her painting and his leather-tufted bar it was a self-made look that took several stiff drinks to get used to. After Daddy passed away, Mother shoved that picture under her bed!

Now do not have an expectation that just because you took lessons from the newly graduated art teacher, you will turn out a Picasso. However, who would want to? That 1938 self-portrait with his eyes offset by half a face in lime green makes me cringe. There is nothing wrong with a good solid oak tree, to begin your hobby.

It is safer and healthier all around, to just stay indoors and paint pictures like the former Presidents do. I chose charcoal art. I tried watercolors, all of mine looked like someone had come into the room and thrown a bucket of water at the picture. The whole scene, slid off the paper, tie dying the carpet under the easel. Oil painting is a future challenge for me, because I have dazzled myself with my charcoal art.

Another disclaimer: It is better not to bring your children in for a critique of your work. I started the charcoals when we were living in Arizona. If they haven't even visited the Hopi House, then they cannot appreciate my rendition. If they have lived in California all their lives, they don't even know what a Saguaro cactus is, much less a pair of cowboy boots.

Now, if I had painted a surfboard bobbing on the ocean wave, I might have gotten a "good job mom", comment. Keep your work close to the vest, unless you are a Past President. They can paint a fence and people will bid millions on it.

When you have raised your family in a typical housing tract neighborhood, you cannot just go wild with paint colors. There are restrictions to the homes exterior color, as mandated earth tone colors.

Then you get a little crazy in retirement with your color choices. Navajo White becomes eggplant purple, haze grey becomes brick red, dusty teal becomes canary yellow; you see where this is going? If the kids want to sell the folks retirement home, the realtor takes a Xanax and calls a painting company to paint it out hospital white if it is to be sold.

Up and until then, it's free range inside the home. I had a home in California that I painted the walls about every three months; it cleaned up nicer, and I could change colors.

I re-arranged furniture with that same frequency. It was better not to give Bruce a glass of wine when he came home tired after work. He has never been a very observant person, and if he had plopped down to sit in his chair and I had moved it, we may have had to pick shards of glass out of him.

I went through many color trends. My mauve period seemed to upset everyone except me. I thought it was fabulous and chic and so California.

My Aunt in Palm Springs did everything herself when she remodeled. She would grab a sledge hammer and knock out a wall, or plaster over her fireplace and mix straw into the plaster to give it a

Palm Springs Indian look. So I tried to keep up with her decorating mania.

The year I painted all of the red brick on the twelve-foot high fireplace the color Mauve was the one I haven't lived down. Everyone thought it was Pepto-Bismol pink, it was NOT! It was Mauve.

I ordered a mauve velvet sectional couch and floral high back wing chairs to complement that! Stunning!! The family took a vote and said the mauve had to go, or I had to go!

I called my Aunt in Palm Springs, and we decided I could re-paint the fireplace "Off White" and put gold glitter in the paint, I jumped on it!

I began wallpapering that house about ten minutes after we signed the loan docs. I started with the family room, continued on to the kitchen, then the master bedroom and the main bathroom. We lived there twenty years and the lady who bought it from us told my neighbor that I was a wallpapering fool.

There were five layers of wallpaper on the main bathroom walls. I had a perfectly good explanation for that; nine people were using that bathroom. If I decided to re-decorate it, it needed to be accomplished in the six hours the kids were at school.

That is just enough time to glue a new layer on; there was no time to steam off old paper. I'm lucky the paper stuck on the wall in the first place. One of our girls took three showers a day; long showers, she inherited from her dad!

When she came home from school, she was straight to the bathroom and water was spraying everywhere. Wallpaper was a gamble with her!

On the occasions that I did re-do that room, it was a melt down to keep her out of there long enough for the fresh layer of paper to dry. My neighbor should never have told me how the buyer felt about my wallpaper; I'm not over it yet!

And, she (that buyer) should also know, as a mother of seven kids, I had another bathroom off the master bedroom with garden tub in it for me. By the time all seven kids took their evening showers for school the next day, there was no hot water for my garden tub. Most of the time it had about a cup and a half of hot water that I used a wash cloth and did a hit and miss job for years!

I never did get around to wallpapering that room!

I painted the dining room gold one time; it turned out mustard in color! I paid so much money for the custom mixed paint job that I decided we could just eat hot dogs in there for a year and give it a chance to grow on us.

And then faux painting came into fashion, and I turned it into a marble wonder. Everyone thought I had a painter do it, and I was using my old make-up sponge wedges, and a clump of leftover tulle from the wedding favors for somebody's wedding. I simply amazed myself.

We recently moved into a house where a young couple had owned it. She obviously called a professional painter and told him to bring the color wheel minus all colors except brown!

Every room was some shade of brown. I was treated for Seasonal Affective Disorder while at that house. I have to disagree with the diagnosis, I think it was burnt brown depression.

Behold All Things New

Anything I buy from a thrift store or consignment store that has a value of greater than one hundred dollars, I will consider a find. Otherwise, I want new. If I want an antique, I want a new reproduction. I want a new car, not the old one; I want a new house, not the old one. I want a new body.

I don't get the car club oldies either. They sit in lawn chairs at a car show and look at their old cars, with new paint on them. They have shelled out upwards of $100k for these new, old cars. The owners hang their heads into the engines and rave about how well this "'ole gal" worked in 1963.

These are people with every ailment in the book, which have electric recliners, electric beds, Jacuzzi spa bathtubs and weekly massages at home. Yet, they cruise down the street or take a car club excursion in a car that does not have a single comfortable aspect to it. The seats are board hard; the windows take brute strength to roll up or down, the doors are so heavy they hit your shinbone while closing and you are in crutches.

It's an amazing concept; I hate old, I hate getting old and I don't want anything old! I think it's all about the potluck dinners and coconut cream pie after the car show concludes.

Young people don't want to get old; they study their wrinkle lines as if leprosy had started on their faces. They discover a grey hair and what do they do? Exactly what our mothers said not to do, they yank it out and ten more grow back. They spend thousands of dollars at the hair salon picking through hair swatches of hair in any color that they can think will make them look younger.

Blue has a defined look, or streaks of char truss pink, give a youthful look on a forty-year-old mother of two. My favorite, Pocahontas jet-black hair; their completion is chalk white and the monthly botox shots have created their own new wrinkle lines.

Movie stars have taken their face lifts to new droop points, botoxed their lips to the size of lemons and when it's all said and done, they age just like the rest of us.

The Botox thing is turning out well, a new generation of angry people who are smiling with frozen facial muscles. Can you see them someday when they are in a nursing home asking some nurse to please help them with something? Nurses don't like to help angry people! Just a thought! They are more inclined to help that dear little old lady with a beautiful white hair and sweet smile.

There is nothing wrong with oldie music though; it is not the lyrics or even the beat for the baby boomer, it's a memory of a time when you were young. For me, opera touches my soul, for Bruce it is fingernails on a chalkboard.

I could never accept Elvis being old, I just put on

his CD of "Don't", and I'm done. If he were alive, a wrinkled old man with his shirt hanging open to grey hairs, I doubt I would swoon the same way.

The new music of today is watching a football game half time show with a kid thrashing and beating on a set of drums and screaming into a microphone. It just "don't do it" for me.

Computers came into our lives with most of us saying, "What do we need that thing for, I have a perfectly good typewriter?" Between learning how to use a computer, applying it to my work and home life and adjusting to every new upload, download, reboot and crash the thing can do, I have made it to the big time.

The Mac....the I Cloud... and the constant state of upgrading, I'm a whiz! The Pièce de résistance is my gold Iphone.   I can text, Skype, and selfie. I'm a guru, computer geek, my life is complete.

 I JUST INFORMED BRUCE I CAN'T LIVE WITHOUT DUAL MONITORS...he just

COLLAPSED! It's taken him thirty years to get me to this point, and it's just too much for him.

How Political Do You Want to Be?

I started out at the P.T.A. meetings and being my kids Home Room Mother, when my little darlings went off to school. I soon realized their forty-three thousand-student district was the Harper Valley P.T.A. Nothing was going to get accomplished on bringing in some desks to my kids classrooms and some new books, if all I was going to do was bake cupcakes for the monthly birthday/holiday party. I ran for the school board. And so began the politics, in my life, Ronnie did it, I thought I could too.

There was no "How to run for your local school board handbook," so as usual, I was winging it. First, I needed to get myself officially on the ballot. The lady at the registrar's office handed me a packet for the required ten thousand voter signatures.

I knew some of the neighbors, some of the kid's friends parents, a few people at church, the lady at the cleaners, and the yardman. (Nope he was not registered with the district). I knew the checker at the grocery store; the pediatrician was on speed dial and everyone in the emergency room at our hospital nearby.

How to get ten thousand signatures? You have to walk the walk and talk the talk. Door to door and one Lions Club to Rotary Club meeting after another and then one day, I reached the required number and flew into that Registrars office expecting a gold medal. She stamped it and said, "Next!"

We needed to design the yard signs, assemble them in the garage and get the kids to staple the yard sticks to the posters without putting their eyes out. Why does a staple gun have to resemble a colt forty-five, this was serious business not the OK Corral? I talked on a radio station; I had to attend debates, I had to face the P.T.A. and the teachers union. I still had to fix dinner!

I was on a TV debate at one point. "Are you a Christian Fundamentalist?" a reporter asked me.

"What? "What's that?" "I am a Christian; I go to church; I have oscillated between Methodist and Presbyterian, but I don't think that makes me mental." "Could you repeat that question?" "The lack of books and no desks in the room, that's my platform." Or maybe that's my shoes, I don't know. Who's bright idea was it to run for anything political?

One of the opponents running against me asked me how I would handle the schools 120 million dollar budget? I gave pause and said "Much like I do ours at home, get a bingo basket, throw the bills in and see what rolls out that we have money in the bank to pay?" "Don't we have an administrative accountant in the district paid to do that?" Next!

Another guy thought he would outwit me and asked me if I were a stay at home mom, what made me think I could run a school district?

I asked him, "When you go home at night, who is there?" He came back with, "My wife" "And you think she is doing what?" "Oh, she's great; she does everything, the bills, the housework, takes care of the kids and me and still looks pretty good, if you know what I mean?" "I think you've answered it for me, the school board position is a piece of cake!"

"However you sir, I think will have to stop off at not only a bakery, but the flower shop and a jewelry store to get through that gem of a question."

I co-hosted a radio show for a while, during the school board campaign. I remember my first time in the booth at the radio station. They put the headset on me and shut the door and turned on a hot red light and left. The door was hermetically sealed and would not open until the 60 minutes was up at the end of the program. Lights would go off, and some frantic little guy was waving at me through a glass window, with that hand sign as the telephone, "pick-up", he was mouthing.

So I answered the phone. "Helloooo, this is Mary, how can I help you?" That was not the question I was not supposed to ask. First give the call signs of the station, KCEO, and then do an ad and then answer. "Well, make up your minds, the phone rings, I answer it."

For months after that radio show gig was over, I answered the home phone with the radio call sign and an ad.

Change is Good, I Want A Tree House

Your tastes change with age. You have prepared tuna casserole and grilled cheese sandwiches for forty years. You are now ready with just the two of you at home to advance on to lobster and drawn butter. Kobe steak for two maybe baked Alaska. Dream on, the doctors tattooed your cholesterol level on your forehead, to remind you of what those foods do to your arteries.

The doctor gives you a pamphlet written by a twenty-two year old dietician who sustains her life on red wine and smelling her dinner plate.

In it, you are instructed not to eat liver, sweetbreads, kidney or brains! I regularly saw those in the surgical suite, and rarely took then home to eat.

You can, however, have a half a cup of tofu and an unbreaded fish fillet, the size of a checkbook. Really girl, we don't even use checkbooks anymore, can I rely on this information?

Cook three ounces of meat (the size of a deck of cards), have you seen any pork chops wrapped in the meat department looking like a deck of cards? Five green olives, that pretty much takes up the whole martini glass and for what? Is that my salad or my appetizer? A half of an English muffin is it possible to eat half of an English muffin? What to do with the other half? It becomes moldy if I leave it for the next week allowance.

Eat a variety of colorful fruits and vegetables; the pamphlet went on to say. Oh good grief, have I ever not seen a colorful fruit or vegetable?

Well, maybe when I clean out the refrigerator and that cucumber is mold grey, and the tomato is black and the orange is green, other than that, fruits and vegetables that I consume remain colorful, I don't need guidance on that.

My exercise is to be in ten-minute bouts, rather than thirty minutes straight. Are you kidding me? Swim for ten minutes, it takes me thirty minutes to get into the suit and forty minutes to get out of a wet one, that is not choosing an activity that I enjoy.

Ten minutes of cross-country skiing was also suggested. Now I want to know where this twenty-two year old dietician resides. It is not in snow country. Getting into the snow garb, putting on the boots and strapping yourself into ski bindings, hardly seems enjoyable for a ten-minute bout. In fact, ten minutes on the snow for me would be from the ski building to the lift chair. It would take me another fifty minutes to ride up the hill, dump off and slid down on my back to the bottom of the hill. These time allotments are completely unrealistic.

Getting my husband to dress up and go out for fine dining is like taking a kid to the Orthodontist and tightening the braces. I have to bribe him with cheese and crackers and guacamole to even get him out the door!

And then, he never buttons the next to the top button on his shirt. He is hot, he is uncomfortable, it is too tight, or somewhere in his adolescence, somebody convinced him that was a sexy look.

A wrinkling old man with grey chest hair does not have the same "Tom Cruise" look with an open shirt! He was quick to point out to me, that at my age, stiletto heels wobbling on the sidewalk doesn't exactly do it either!

I digress, back to the tree house. I could be hallucinating from lack of food, but I don't think so. Some people can live in the same house, with the same furniture from the 1960 look, that same wallpaper print on the kitchen walls that the former owner had and go no further than their county line.

They live and they die in the same spot; their headstones are in the garage ready for the final dates.

I have reached a point in time after living in the track home project for twenty five years, a condominium filled with toxic mold, a new house and an old house, I would like an out of the ordinary home experience. I am leaning toward a tree house.

I thought for a while a remodeled caboose on a train track headed out of the country would be nice, but the logistics drove Bruce crazy. I saw a refurbished airplane shell that had possibilities, but it was hanging over a cliff on an earthquake fault.

My cabin in the woods idea in Alaska had to be re-thought with the outhouse, I would just go so far camping. I think the underground cave dwellers need some serious psychological help; they could not give me an underground mud house in the Mohave Desert.

But a tree house that suits me to a tee. As long as it can be new, look new, have rain and steam shower, full kitchen, dishwasher, laundry room, king bed, and windows everywhere. I want a hidden staircase as in the Anne Frank house; I couldn't navigate up the hidden staircase, but the loft would be good storage for my thrift shop finds. I am looking for it; it's out there somewhere.

I won't go as far as that guy in the Rain Forest, living in a tree stump, but I would invite him over for a break in the decor, maybe offer him a real chair to sit in. Of course if he insisted on wearing fresh moss on his head, I'd have to think about an overnighter.

He doesn't impress me making his berry fruit jam with his dirty feet either. Come to think of it, I think he's better off staying in the stump.

There's probably a moonshiner's still in his cave, how would anybody get through a rain soaked winter with a cotton ball, some Vaseline and a box of kitchen matches? All he eats is berries, and a dried mushroom, that's diarrhea all winter! That's butt rash; that then breaks down to a tunneled ulceration.

Ahhh yup; its time for the wound vac! His only pain relief would be the clear "shine" in the Mason jar; there's no numbing ointment in the Rain Forest.

Rx From Me To You

The wound care nurse in me stays although I'm officially retired from nursing. I always think of the wound vac. It is a machine and a bandage all in one, put it over the wound and suck out the infection. Pictures and humor have a way of sucking all the infection out of our struggles, unless I'm taking them, then life is a blur!

We capture all of fun moments in the pictures we take. When we were in the Grand Canyon, Bruce, and I stopped on the walkway; we both gasped at the same time at a man who was on the backside of the railing with clearly marked signs, "do not step over the railing." His new bride was taking a picture of him. She kept saying, "I can't get all of you in the picture can you step back a little?"

There is not much a retired nurse can do for a guy who steps back over the edge of the steep side of the Grand Canyon and falls into the Colorado River. I yelled; Bruce yelled, the park service lady was hysterical; she pulled her gun out of the holster. Maybe she was going to shoot him and relieve him of pain on the way down.

All I could think of during the time he was standing there and the time it took to get him back over the railing to safety was....he wouldn't be a candidate for the wound vac. By the time, he would have bounced off rocks six thousand feet down; there wouldn't be any muscle mass to connect the wound vac to him. That's a shame, just bloody bones! Bruce said to me, "Are you thinking that sick wound vac stuff again?"

We have been taking pictures and documenting our lives from birth to death. I admired the mothers who organized their slides and labeled them with who, what, when and where on a tiny one inch by one piece of cardboard around the slide.

They carefully slid each slide into a plastic canister to be ready for the slide show. It's just that a three-year-old thinks those canisters are fun and set them up like building blocks. They tumble over, and one thousand indiscernible pictures become a massive puzzle on the floor. Do you kill the kid? Do you cry? I just scooped them up with the pancake spatula and piled them into a box that I would get back to one day.

The slides became photo albums. There are mothers with three hundred albums assembled of every movement the baby made from its first breath until the wedding day. Those albums are leather bound and gold embossed and would take at least a year and a half to thumb through them nonstop, to even begin to see all the pictures.

Those are the scrape-booker gals; they are stores dedicated to scrapbooking, with stickers and supplies for these women to spend on average, about four hundred dollars per book.

It's a hand off memory, only by the time the mother has spent $120,000 on these albums, the children have grown up to a digital CD collection.

Now the entire album pictures have to be scanned and burned on CD, then burn onto DVDs, transferred to a pdf file and off loaded or uploaded or downloaded to a burned disk. At fifty-five dollars each to transfer, burn and create the CD, the collection now is at $135,000.

Those mother's proudly wrapped the newly formatted collection all up in a black, nylon CD case holder, zippered closed with mini padlock. Then handed them over to the child to whom this loving investment had been made.

That kid promptly said to her, "Mom you are so outdated, you know you can put that on a thumb drive and I don't have to have all of those dumb CD's!"

If that same mother happened to take movies, she started out with a jerky 8 mm, transferred that to a CD and then DVD. That changed to digital movie on a memory chip that she lost in the bowels of her purse. That chip was never found; she threw it away mistakenly in a wad of Kleenex.

She could have prevented that and put the whole thing in the cloud! However, if she forgets the password, or hits delete, $150,000 out the door.

Invariably every kid says, "Mom why didn't you take more pictures of me?" "Well, for Pete sakes, add it up." " We had seven kids!" "You do the math!"

Smack Talk

First it was, "I hear what you are saying", then it was "Bitch'in", then it was "don't be a spaz"....now if you are trying to get a point across, you are "Smack talking". That used to be my favorite cereal!

I had to call my youngest daughter and have her define a hash tag to me; I thought it was another pot thing and at this point, who cares? "So I send a message to you and don't sign my name or Mom, just #tiredtoday."

"Got it!" Well, maybe not. If hash tags are to help people find out what others are saying and then it is a public conversation, I'd better not, #constipated.

This is not a new trend meant for Dad, he will hash tag his thoughts on highway construction, stop signs, red lights and I will have to bail him out of jail.

The kids don't want to hear about history or anything we did in the past, so what do they devise? "Throwback Thursday", post a bunch of old pictures of yesteryear.

I'm devising a new social throwback, "Throwback Sunday, CALL YOUR MOTHER." Their cell phones are an appendage to their body, yet on the weekends, they put them into some holding pattern, they see a call coming in or the text, from their parents but they ignore it. So "Throwback Sunday" or parents will "Throwout the kids!"

Don't think I don't know what LOL means; I'm still working on LMAO. IANAL!

I opened a Twitter account...I don't know where it goes or who it goes to. I've watched it for three years, and I have two followers. There's a corner of the computer screen that says, "trending", maybe Lady GAGA will follow me, if I click on her. But then what is "Pink Trout Lady" going to mean to her from me? That was the only name they would give me for my account. Apparently, my name Mary is too common.

I can't even get my head around Instagram! A bunch of kids prettied up some photos, and video's to put in their social media page and they got a billion dollars for it! I've been decorating the house, the yard, the kids, and the dog for thirty years, and I haven't gotten a buck 98!

One of my friends is refusing to get in on this new world of social exchange. She keeps her landline phone and a flip phone with no texting.

Her grandkids are shaming her with their technology, "Nana, you could have found me at the ballpark, if you'd had the school app!." She comes back strong to them, "Don't you worry darling, I'll drive this campus round and round, before you see me app'ing!"

There is new legislation on the horizon to keep children from bullying each other. I wonder what these young folks want to do with the little boys new craze at school. "Balls punching!"

When my husband was in junior high, the boys would sock each other on the upper arm, "Go ahead hit it harder, I can take it!"

This new craze is way beyond that. "Go ahead, hit me in the balls, harder!" They come waddling out maintaining they have a wedgie and their mothers drive on down the street, talking on the earpiece of their cell phone, with no clue the child's testicles are swelling to the size of a grapefruit.

Beats my son, stuffing dried beans up his nose!

The Final Will

It has finally happened, the doctor's office, the hospital and my spa pedicurist all are requiring an Advanced Directive. I have pushed this off now for thirty years; it started out "My Last Will and Testament' and now it is a microchip implanted in the underarm cellulite hanging from my body. I have had to specify what I want done with my used and unused parts.

This is not my parents will or lack thereof, I have to sign up for advanced planning classes. Then start the action plan. This is all accomplished on the website, it prompts you through the questions. Let's get started!

The first question on this website asked me what was most important in my life. It then gave an example of what someone thought was most important to them.

The prompt said; Jorge wants to see his niece get married. I don't even know Jorge, how is this applicable? I've probably spent forty years asking that question. I have finally decided it is to get through one day and not feel guilty if I'd rather have pie for breakfast.

The next question could have approached me with more sensitivity. Are there some health situations that would make your life not worth living?

Well, an asthma attack in the checkout lane is not a pretty sight. No one says, "Oh, please, you go ahead of me," after that commercial where the guy stepped ahead of a man in line and won a million dollars. Those in line are more inclined to say, "Die lady, I might be the next winner!"

The next question was a doosie, asking me if I thought about my health and my health situation and then the audacity to ask me how do I feel about that?

This has got to be a thirty year old drafting these questions.

You start thinking about your health when it's going downhill, not when you can run the five hundred mile sprint. And your health situation that only means you are dealing with a non-working something somewhere in your body.

If your lips are the size of a lemon on your face because you botoxed them weekly; and the formaldehyde has frozen in place, that is your fault. The only health situation is you have embalmed yourself before your time.

However, your shoulder tendon thinned with age, and it snapped leaving your arm dangling and unable to use, is a real health situation.

Asking me how I feel about it, I can go generational superficial and say:

"I like my feet; I'm better off than the bunion lady." I think I have a strong heart, although my kids have bruised the heck out of it. I have great blood pressure; I know I die without it. My nails have ridges, and I have age spots that depress me.

My asthma is in a lethal state, so my doctor indicates. However, her asthma is too, and we seem to be chugging right along. I monitor her; she monitors me.

I could hardly wait for the fourth question; this one took some in-depth research. Do I remember seeing someone on TV who was very sick or dying? Think about what went well and did not go well?

Ok, let me think about this...on the TV show, "I Love Lucy" she could have died in that tub of grapes and with her red hair that would have been a sight to behold in the coffin. When "General Hospital" had someone dying, they usually came back to the show the next season. I guess that went well. Walter was terminally ill with cancer the entire time "Breaking Bad" was on the air. He died in his meth lab, with a smile on his face that was what he wanted.

I tell you for the country being super politically correct, asking me if I want to end my life the same purposeful way I lived it, made me wonder who wrote this stuff? Is this anti-NRA politics sliding into the questionnaire? I came in with a bang; I'll go out with a bang?

There hasn't been any purpose to my life. It has been a mad dash to stay ahead of bill collectors, the toilets being clogged, the appliances working through Christmas, the cars running, and remembering to take the one pill to keep myself alive.

Good grief, it was now time to fill in the required forms:

1. The genealogy record of your family dating back to the beginning of time.

Not a problem, I'll cut and paste the information I did on that thirty years ago.

2. The confidential record of your pap smears.

I can't provide that information, that area atrophied and after age 65 it was all discarded.

3. Your current employment status.

Would I be filling out an advanced directive if my career were in upward mobility?

4. What do you want done with your remains?

Now you are getting to the crux of why I cemetery cruise on our trips.

At this point in time, I would like to be placed next to John Wayne in the New Port Beach, California Cemetery by the sea. He is an unmarked grave, should be easy to find, and the view is spectacular.

Or, my second choice, next to the big bell at the Valley of the Temples Cemetery in Hawaii. I'm not Hawaiian, I know, but I have all of Israel Kamakawiow's CD's, if that helps.

It was recently on the news, that all the cemeteries are filling up, so if none of this works out, put me on a piece of ice and float me out to the polar bears.

Having completed this process, the paperwork is signed, notarized, filed with the department of Agriculture or whatever. I have given permission to unplug me, after I have my morning coffee.

Would you believe this, there are seventy million other seniors ahead of me who cannot get through the prompts in the website. A facilitator has determined the site has crashed and she being a "Y generational," needs additional coaching.

All of my documentation is frozen in cyberspace. I can see the handwriting on the wall; I'm not going to get my pedicure or see the Chaplain, until this site works.

www.ingramcontent.com/pod-product-compliance
Lightning Source LLC
LaVergne TN
LVHW051824080426
835512LV00018B/2721